POLITICAL DEVELOPMENT IN INDIA

By the same author

Indian Administration
The Evolution of Indian Administration
The General Election in India
Public Administration (co-author)
Government Through Consultation
The Administrative Reforms Commission
Local Government in India
The Study of Public Administration in India (edited)
The Civil Service in Great Britain
President's Rule in India
State Government in India
Teaching of Public Administration in India (edited)
Public Administration in India :
Management of Change
Open Government in India
Indian Parliamentary System
Administrative Reforms in India
Electoral Politics in the National Metropolis
Comparative Government and Politics
Rural Development in India (in press)

Political Development in India

SHRIRAM MAHESHWARI
Professor of Political Science & Public Administration
Indian Institute of Public Administration
New Delhi

CONCEPT PUBLISHING COMPANY, NEW DELHI

First Published 1984

Shriram **Maheshwari** (*b.* 1931-)

Published by
Naurang Rai
Concept Publishing Company
H-13 Bali Nagar
NEW DELHI-110015 (India)

Printed in India by
Bharti Printers
at Mohan Printing Corporation
DELHI-110007

Dedicated
to
the ever-sweet memory
of
my nephew
SURESH KUMAR
(22 February 1960—7 November 1983)

Preface

THE Indian political system is witnessing changes of far-reaching significance since the seventies, and the pace of development has further accelerated in the eighties. Ever since the 1971 election, the voter's verdict has been clear and decisive. The other political forces were made to eat the dust, and Indira Gandhi and her Congress Party received overwhelming support in the election of 1971. This election was of historic significance for her, for she was then a relatively less known and established politician, and on the verdict of this election depended her political career. The period between 1971 and the next election of 1977 was extraordinarily crowded and the verdict of 1977 was most loud and unambiguous—the Congress Party was for the first time ignominously defeated at the centre replaced as it was by the Janata Party. The Janata Party, however, proved to be too disunited and went out of office in 1979 ; Charan Singh was the caretaker prime minister until 1980 when the voter paved the way for the return of the prodigious Indira Gandhi, by electing her party with a thumping majority.

In 1971, 1977 and 1980 the electorate has thus acted firmly and conclusively, speaking in one voice, as it were. When the next election is round the corner a question of interest is : will the voter be equally emphatic in his endorsement ? The voter's choice will naturally be influenced by very many factors at work both at the conscious and sub-conscious levels.

The present work is a modest attempt to analyse the several facets of the fast changing political scenario in India with a view to gaining a sharper understanding of the political system and its dynamics, and recommending, where necessary, corrective measures too. The environmental pressures on politics have been analysed and the interface with economics highlighted. All these and many more aspects have been discussed under the title of political development recognising fully well that some atleast could perhaps appropriately be said to signify the onset of a process of decay in the national political life. The major problem-areas have been identified and corrective plans suggested. India's two foremost problems are a decline in public ethics and an explosion of its population, and both can be tackled if the political leadership is firmly prepared to take hard decisions : the soft options are apt to be unavailing.

The idea of attempting a book of this nature emerged when the author first started teaching the course on Indian political system in the Institute's Advanced Professional Programme in Public Administration. It was most stimulating to discuss the subject with the APPPA students : the classroom was truly the laboratory of the book. The author sincerely thanks all his APPPA students with whom the subject used to be discussed.

The author is indebted to a large number of politicians, civil servants, journalists and others who were good enough to discuss the subject with him and thus to share their knowledge. An assurance of complete confidentiality forbids the author from thanking them publicly. Nevertheless, he is deeply beholden to them. Many others might be thanked publicly. The author must very warmly thank R.K. Trivedi, Chief Election Commissioner of India, for having made himself available for discussion on certain matters. He is indebted to S. Sahay, Delhi Editor, *The Statesman*, and Girilal Jain, Editor, *The Times of India*, who were kind enough to spend a considerable chunk of their time with him in analysing some of the major concerns of Indian politics. T.N. Chaturvedi has always been a source of encouragement and inspiration : the author's warm thanks go to him. The author would like to tender his thanks to Vidya Charan Shukla, the former central minister and presently the Member of Parliament, for his advice, help and encouragement in the writing of this book. For views and opinions, however, the author alone is responsible.

30 June 1984 SRM
Rath Yatra

Acknowledgements

GRATEFUL acknowledgement is made of the permission of the editors for the reproduction and use of the following articles in the present volume :

1. *Indian Journal of Public Administration*, for
   (1) 'The Political Executive and the Permanent Executive', Vol. XXVI, No. 3, (July-September 1980).
   'Indian Federal System : Distortions and Correctives', Vol. XXIX, No. 4 (October-December 1983).

2. *Legislative Studies Quarterly*, for
   'The Constituency Linkage of National Legislators in India', Vol. 1, No. 3, August 1976.

3. *Changing Contours : A Political Study*,
   (Secunderabad, M. Venkatarangaiya Foundation, 1982), for 'The Indian Politician : Then and Now.'

Contents

1

POLITICAL DEVELOPMENT IN INDIA
An over-view

INDIAN POLITY or political system is of late finding itself under a new level of stress and, that too, from several quarters. One may even say that it is at the cross-roads at present, and which turn it is likely to take in the near future is not very certain. A dispassionate analysis of Indian politics is thus crucially important to help influence its future course.

ACHIEVEMENTS

A study of the country's political system, not unnaturally, may generate divergent views but one must look at it in a perspective. We Indians, are often criticised for being more critical of India than we need be, and such a cultural trait warns us to keep our perspective right and undimmed. The political system has to its credit many gains and achievements the significance of which may not be minimised. India, today, is an important member of the international community, and its counsels receive serious attention in the various capitals of the world. It is one of the pioneers of the non-alignment movement, and today the non-aligned bloc claims a membership of no less than 100 nation-states in the world, which is a testimony to the vision and leadership in India provided at that critically important early stage. Besides, India has managed its economy fairly well ; at any rate, its record in this field has not been very disappointing as compared to many other developing countries even if it is not adjudicated as being very adequate. India ranks as the tenth most highly industrialised country in the world. One should also not overlook the fact that while some Latin American countries are witnessing runaway inflation, India has succeeded in bringing it down from the two digit figure to one digit one, which itself is a notable feat.

Furthermore, the infrastructure which India has succeeded in developing is bound to attract the admiration of the whole world.

Today, India has a vast network of scientific and technological institutions and it possesses the third largest scientific and technological manpower in the world. Educational expansion has been equally impressive. Many of our scientists and technologists—indeed, experts in all areas of knowledge—are occupying responsible positions even in the developed countries of the world. Indeed, the country is not deficient in any field of skills and knowledge. The transport and communication system is well developed and so are other infrastructural facilities.

No less significant have been the political gains of India registered since 1950, the base line. The very unbroken continuity of the polity is itself an achievement : an aspect which readily acquires vividness and colour when remembered that in the Third World Indian Constitution is the oldest one, and what is even more creditable, the constitution is a *functioning* one. Secondly, in spite of occasional ups and downs, India has enjoyed a fairly stable government both at the centre and in the states since the commencement of the constitution. What is most remarkable in the Third World, India has established a convention of constitutionalism in the matter of change of government : the change is peaceful and strictly through the ballot. There have been three such occasions at the centre—in 1977, 1979[1] and 1980—and each time the successor government was installed peacefully and in accordance with the constitution. This has provided the necessary environment for implementation of successive five-year plans and, besides, accorded operational legitimacy to the constitutional arrangements of the land. Above all, there has been a steady deepening of the political awareness of the people, and the democratic institutions have generally taken roots in the country at all levels.

FAILURES

This is not to suggest that the Indian balance sheet has all gains to its credit, and failures and inadequacies have been practically nil or insignificant. India's achievements have certainly been many and impressive, but all the same have proved to be inadequate, and not very wider-ranging. The nation could have registered much greater

1. Inviting Charan Singh to form the government at the Centre and letting his ministry continue even on his failure to gain the confidence vote of the Lok Sabha raised some constitutional controversy, but does not weaken the thrust of the argument.

progress and in many more areas of life. It is well to look at the side of the medal also.

India's single greatest failing has been in that sphere which imparts completeness to life : the sphere of public ethics. There has been nearly total neglect of civic and moral education of the people, and a whole generation has grown to adulthood without it. Morality is plainly at its lowest ebb in the India of today, and hardly any walk of life remains unsullied by this deterioration. There is wide-spread lack of public honesty, commitment, sincerity and integrity in whatever we are doing, which has sometime made others call us hypocrites, India presently functions in a state of moral anaesthesia.

A dwindling concern for the nation as a whole is another most distressing feature of the contemporary life. India was more of a nation during the British period than today[2], and of late the process of unmaking a nation may seem to be more in evidence than that of making a nation. Besides, a loss of broader vision, imaginative insight, statesmanly foresight, sagacity too, has come to be clearly and painfully discerned in the thoughts and actions of leadership, political, or otherwise. The parochialism was always a latent factor in the Indian psyche, but remained sub-merged during the first decade and half of India's independence. With the disappearance of Pandit Jawaharlal Nehru and of leadership trained under the Gandhi-era the Age of Broad Minds came to an end, succeeded by progressively poorer replacements. Today, small men are seen strutting about casting long shadows in most walks of life, whereas the really good and great are producing short shadows.

These are the larger failures impinging on all walks of life. One may proceed further to chronicle, even though briefly, the ill successes on the purely material plane.

India's single greatest failure has been its incapacity to control its population whereas it ought to have been considered as the biggest problem before the nation. The fast increasing numbers not only neutralise the gains from developmental efforts which have been under way since the time of Independence but also impose a heavy

2. When Surendranath Banerjee wrote his reminiscences in 1925 the title he chose was *A Nation in Making*. The great public leader's contention, by implication, was that India was not yet an integrated nation but the process towards it had well begun.

strain on the country's limited resources.[3] Closely following is the distressingly wide economic anomalies in the society. There is more inequality in India today than ever in the past, and this owes itself directly to the model of growth and the economic policies which it has pursued. Even after the implementation of successive five-year plans, the purchasing power is concentrated in ten per cent or so of the population, and the pattern of industrial production is largely dictated by such an unnaturally small number. Nearly half of the country's population continues to live below the poverty line. India is a land where extreme affluence and extreme poverty co-exist, and even man's conscience has ceased to react to such distortions.

PROFILES OF POLITICS

Having discussed, very briefly, the larger social failures one may now move to the field of politics. But here the pattern of discussion would be to analyse the functions of the political system, delineate the major features characterising its functioning and then to highlight the problems it is afflicted with.

The functions of the political system had been woven and coded in the freedom movement of India and are articulated in the Objectives Resolution adopted by the Constituent Assembly on 22 January 1947. The Objectives Resolution promised, among others, to guarantee and secure 'to all the people of India justice, social, economic and political ; equality of status, of opportunity, and before the law ; freedom of thought, expression, belief, faith, worship, vocation, association and action.'[4] These are orchestrated in the preamble, fundamental rights and the directive principles of state policy of the Constitution. The political system, thus, derives its terms of reference, so to day, from the Constitution, but one must not forget that the latter also leaves options and choices : the political leaders may emphasize certain aspects and keep others at a low

3. According to the 1981 census, India's population stands at 684 million, and the increase since 1951 is as under :

Year	*Percentage of increase since the previous census*
1951	13.3
1961	21.5
1971	24.8
1981	24.8

During 1951-81 the population of India increased from 361 million to 686 million, the compound annual growth rate being 2.15 per cent.

4. See B. Shiva Rao (ed) ; *The Framing of India's Constitution*, Vol. II, New Delhi, Indian Institute of Public Administration, 1967, p. 4.

key. This is another way of saying that the operating reality need not necessarily and in all its details conform to the constitutional values. But at the same time, the gap must not be a cause of embarrassment to the system.

The politics under the Constitution of India (1950), understandably, marked strong continuities with the past, and this continued to be the case until the fourth general election (1967) though the constitutional provisions of periodic elections based on universal franchise contained seeds of change and transformation. The political leadership of the freedom movement and hence of the Gandhi era was gradually thinning out for a variety of reasons—such as death, defeat in elections or demands of other dimensions—making room for new elements which the general elections based on adult suffrage began to throw up and whose strongest qualification lay in their acceptability by the newly enfranchised sections of the society. These sections, it may be noted, are those which have traditionally been occupying lower rungs of the economic ladder and are also, generally, illiterate. Indeed, under the impact of general elections held on adult franchise there has been a gradual but distinct shift, both spatial and vertical, of political power, but it was in the general election of 1966-67 that these new forces finally registered their ascendancy and triumph. The urban based, upper caste dominated politics was getting increasingly vernacularised and thus becoming much more broad-based admitting within its fold vast numbers of hither to untapped groups and sections of the population. Simultaneously, a distinct process of ruralisation of Indian politics has been in the offing : agriculturists have of late emerged as the largest occupational group in the Parliament.

The year 1967 may thus rightly be said to constitute a Great Divide in Indian political history. The general election held in that year signified a nearly complete disappearance of the older leadership and heralded the full emergence of the new one ; and as a result, the representatives became very nearly like those they represent. This, as already mentioned, was inherent in the system. Under the constitution the source of political power became voting rights and the majority and as such the hitherto neglected groups, which are economically backward, generally illiterate but which nevertheless constitute majority in the country were bound to come increasingly into power—or, at any rate, to hold balance of power in the immediate future. The fourth general election was followed and accompanied by some unusual features. Jawaharlal Nehru had passed away in the interval between the third and the fourth general elections and his place was filled up by leadership which had no such charisma, atleast to begin with. It was also a period of economic hardship, for the country was in the grip of a severe drought. India announced devaluation of its currency which hit its economy very adversely. The Second Five Year Plan (1956-61) characterised as it was by its industry orientation and huge public outlay had injected not inconsiderable black money into the market. The sebsequent elections have dutifully reinforced these trends and made interface between politics and money power move intimate.

While a person ready to make sacrifices joined politics during the freedom struggle, in Independent India politics became election-based : it is through election that one now graduates into politics. Elections, it is common knowledge, are becoming increasingly expensive, much beyond the capacity of most politicians, which inevitably makes them dependent on money bags. In short, politics which has emerged is linkage politics. The adoption of planning and of mixed economy pattern of development meanwhile has greatly expanded the patronage of the state, and the businessman, actual or aspiring, needs the politician to help him in getting licences, permits and quotas and other benefits from the government of the day, and in the process creating relationship of inter-dependencies and mutual benefits.

In short, electoral politics was beginning to produce its own logic and it became the seed bed of corruption involving the politician, the fund-givers and even the voters. Politics has been fast becoming amoral, if not immoral also at times.[5]

Being the ruling party, the Congress Party shapes and controls the country's tone and pattern of politics, and it itself was undergoing a fundamental change in its internal composition. Each election brought in new members ; so did the two splits of 1969 and 1978. Its strategies of working and orientations deeply changed. But this is not to imply that other parties have stayed completely unchanged.

5. This kind of situation had emerged by the late sixties when the atmosphere became thick with talks about corruption in politics and administration. The probes made against two politicians, one being a state chief minister and other a central minister, served to confirm the existence of wide spread corruption in the public life of the country. Yet the overriding belief at the time was that these lapses but aberrations and would pass away. K.D. Malviya affair was investigated by Justice S.R. Das. See *Lok Sabha Debates* Third Series, Vol. XIX No. 4, 17 August 1963, Col. 964-5. The charges against Pratap Singh Kairon (Chief Minister of Punjab) were examined by the S.R. Das Commission of Inquiry ; sec *The Report of the Commission of Inquiry* ; (New Delhi, Manager of Publications, 1964).

Political parties in India display an extraordinary degree of homogeneity in their electoral behaviour : rigging of election, booth capturing, intimidation of voters and recourse to violence, mobilisation of anti-social elements, and so on have become an integral part of India's contemporary political culture. Moreover, the Janata Party, which remained in power at the centre during 1977-79, was hopelessly ridden with personal and factional rivalries and divergent aims among its members. In the manner of its functioning it was little different from the Congress Party which it replaced scoring massive victory in the value-laden election of 1977. Early in 1979, the Janata Party fell under the weight of its own contradictory pressures, paving the way for return to power of Indira Gandhi in 1980. It would not be very wrong to say that all ruling parties are reproducing the Congress Party's characteristic attributes in themselves. Politicians in India seem to look so much like, for they are essentially the products of a common process which is autonomous of them. Political parties in a competitive system initially encounter a tension between their ideological goals and office (or power) goals, but steadily the goal of office comes to critically determine the party decisions and behaviour, which means that the structure of political opportunities within a political system affects, its funding its capacity to attract voters, and so on. This happens because political parties compete to control, a process which they did not establish and which, moreover, could go on without them. 'Better led than dead', or even 'lesser red than dead' seems to be an apparently unavoidable option for parties including even the fiercely leftist ones.

IMPACT OF NEW FORCES

Consequently, the political system in India is of late finding itself under mounting stress, and what is more, there does not appear to be any signs of pressures getting abated in the near furture. First, the country's politics seeks to entrust more and more activities and functions to the state. This is despite the fact that it is, in open, overly critical of bureaucratic incompetence and corruption. The politician in India has a wonderful capacity to live with contradictions, and thus while disparaging public administration he continues to burden it with new responsibilities. The state is being looked upon for doing even the most trivial things and as a result, areas of voluntary efforts and cooperation are getting consistently shrunk and shrivelled for want of support and nourishment. Second, there is too much of demand being made on the country's political system with little attention being given to its capabilities and capacities. The consequence is that it has today become nearly unmanageable in terms of the system's handling capacity. In the third place, all sectors and layers of this huge chunk of mankind living in India have become increasingly politicised though not equally and in well rounded form but some have become more vocal and command bargaining power disproportionate to their numerical strength or even to their political significance thanks to periodic elections held on adult suffrage. Politics is kept fanned up incessantly and today no decision is believed to carry finality with it. Fourthly, the politics which is practised in the country has become growingly ruthless and normless, and a belief has gone round to the effect that what matters in the world is succeess in total disregard to how it is achieved and by what means. Political violence has by now established itself as an integral part of the contemporary political culture. How different all this is from the purity of means and the cult of non-violence preached and practised by Mahatma Gandhi. Fifthly, the country's politics has been becoming increasingly ahistorical, being conducted too much in terms of the present and heavily discounting the future. In the process, it has singularly failed to examine the emerging problems in a long-term perspective. It has not been able to strike a balance between the 'unity' and 'diversity' factors thereby giving a free reign to diversity. Indeed, the contemporary politics of India is vividly centrifugal and fragmentary. India is acclaimed as a country characterised by unity amidst diversity, but little effort has been made to promote and reinforce unity. Rather, it is engaged in a rather risky game of institutionalisation of diversity with the consequence that, today, claiming a separate and distinct identity has become an ambition of an ever-increasing number of people in the country. And, very often they succeed too. Sixthly, politics has become increasingly agitational, and what is more an impression has got created that it pays also—or, as some one said, it alone pays these days ! It is an indication of the times that political crimes including minor crimes have generally come to be treated rather lightly—and are even sometimes ignored or condoned. Seventhly, a steep deterioration in moral values also marks the politics of the country. Many, especially those who have entered it in the recent past, do not seem to have adequate preparation for the profession of politics or a spirit of social commitment. Generally, dedication and social purposiveness are low in a sizeable number of politicians whatever be their public postures.[6] Political opportunism is a widespread evil debasing the country's politics. Widespread existence of political corruption may be cited as the eighth, but most serious feature of India's politics. Its roots lie in the electoral politics but have been fanned up by the governmental power of regulation and control of the nation's economy as well as phenomenal increase in public expenditure. The prevalence of widespread corruption among politicians is eloquently confirmed by each of the twenty-two commissions of inquiry set up by the centre and the states against individual politicians from time to time since Independence. Another finding of these commissions is the growing collusion between the minister and the civil servants in a large variety of shady activities. The emerging corruption is not necessarily in the form of money : it may be patronage. It is thus not very incorrect to say that a disturbingly large number of politicians and civil servants have learnt by now to accommodate each other in a wide variety of matters at the expense of public interest.

6. "Could you please give some reasons why you have joined politics" was a question which the present author put to the various candidates seeking election to the Delhi Metropolitan Council in 1977. Some of their replies are interesting and are being reproduced :

"I just joined ; I did not plan the political career for myself. I was a public debater, which brought me to politics. But I have not regretted having come to politics. Financially, it has damaged me enormously. I have joined the Janata Party as I want to prevent bogus people from usurping the Janata Party. I am fighting against forces which rely upon falsehood and treachery. I am contesting the election with the J.P. spirit : do not cling to power but fight for truth."

"I have seen my father serving the people through the medium of politics. Unless one has power to get certain things done one can't serve the people."

"In order to be effective in his work one has got to have political power. This is why I am contesting elections."

"I was and am interested in social work. During the course of my social work I had some experiences. Social problems can be solved only politically ; hence I decided to come directly into politics. In 1962 I was nominated to the New Delhi Municipal Committee. My experience of NDMC was very satisfying. A social worker can maximise his effort by coming to politics."

"A desire to serve the people has brought me to politics".

"I have joined politics to help the poor and weaker sections of the society."

"I came to politics to solve the problems of the poor labourers living in the area."

"I want to serve the people."

"I am a trader as well as a social worker. I joined politics to solve people's problems."

"I have joined politics and sought election at the request of the people."

Last but quite worrying is the ubiquitousness of politics in the India of today. While policy decisions are bound to be affected by the party ideology enunciated in the election manifesto, individual decisions must be based on merits and in national interest—as against party interest. The present obsession with the ensuing elections mars public decision making in all spheres. Politics is ubiquitous in another sense also. Politics has become so possessive that today it is apparently prepared to accept no boundary : with utmost obstinacy it continues to expand its area, and today it has come to project itself in most spheres of life with the consequence that there does not exist any de-politicised sector of activities in the country. It seems to pervade most areas of life : it superimposes itself on almost everything. Any one aspiring to be of some consequence in the country in any area of life must have political levers. An effect of such all sprawling politics is that it is stultifying and stunting the autonomous growth of other wings of life.

(*Contd.*)

"My desire to solve the problems facing the Muslims has brought me to active politics. It is only through elections that problems can be solved. Politics gives power to me."

"I was persuaded to join politics. Nor did I wish to contest the election. I was persuaded to fight."

These make very interesting reading. First, all candidates proclaim to serve the people. If such a view is genuine the country should indeed consider itself to be very fortunate, having a very large number of selfless citizens committed to public weal. Secondly, even persons engaged in social work feel that politics makes them more effective. The reader can draw has own inferences from the above replies, but two observations may not be very irrelevant here. Indian politics is deeply intermingled with hypocrisy, and a politician cannot publicly give up the posture of saintliness. Secondly, whatever may be its criticism, in India political power commands enormous respect and attention in terms of producing result and therefore, almost everyone seems to be running after it. (See S.R. Maheshwari : *Electoral Politics in the National Metropolis*, New Delhi, Ritu Publishers, 1982, pp. 88-9).

2

THE POLITICIAN

THE POLITICIAN in India is a contribution of the British rule, though unintended in the sense that his emergence was not contemplated much less planned by the colonial rulers. He was a by-product of the Raj : the British set up a system of government hitherto unknown to India and adopted policies which released forces and impulses fostering the coming of the politician. When they, for instance, decided in 1835 to instal English as the official language of governance and made provision for its teaching in India, the seed was sown and it was only a matter of time for the politician to emerge. The English educated Indians sought government employment, and the first politician in India emerged to articulate this demand, becoming in the process an advocate of Indians' increased entry into the country's public services. The Indian National Congress, established in 1885, was primarily an employment-seeking organisation, to begin with.

The first generation politician had certain attributes worth noting. He was as a rule an English-knowing Indian hailing mostly from Bengal and Bombay engaged in one of the modern professions—law or teaching or journalism. He wore western dress, conversed in English and was an amateur in the sense that politics was his pre-occupation, not occupation. The style of his politics reflected correctly his own aspirations and suited admirably the exigencies of the times. He would make petitions and requests to the raj to seek acceptance of his demands and would never think of a goal or the means by which to attain it which was not strictly constitutional. These politicians were elitists in the double sense : they came from selected regions of India—mostly Bengal and Bombay—and what is more, from selected upper classes—Bhadralok of Bengal and Parsis and Chitpawan Brahmins of Bombay.

The profile of the politician was changing, and the next landmark, easily, is the famous Partition of Bengal in 1905, which had, among others, the effect of making politics much more widespread by recruiting persons from newer regions and much larger band of the society. For the first time students were enrolled into politics. What is more, the style of politics also became more diversified and even did not completely eschew occasional agitations and political violence. Shortly after, Balgangadhar Tilak played a pioneering role in making politics broader in terms of its support-structure and the hitherto elitist Indian National Congress a mass party. Much as Tilak's contribution is to Indian politics, it however continued to exhibit more continuities with its past than discontinuities.

It was given to Mohandas Karamchand Gandhi, who returned to India in 1915 after earning a name in South Africa, to revolutionise politics and impart it an image which has remained associated with it ever since, atleast in the outward form. Gandhi inherited a kind of club which the Indian National Congress was at the time but very quickly he converted it into a mass political party penetrating into even the far-flung villages and inducting into it persons from various socio-economic strata of the society. Gandhi recruited into politics persons from all strata of life including the middle and lower middle classes, for he had a message for every one—farmers, artisans, women, students, lawyers, doctors, teachers, harijans, industrialists, factory workers, etc. Gandhi extended his catchment area to induct women who joined the nationalist movement for the first time. Under the call of non-cooperation movement many gave up their vocations and plunged themselves into the national struggle for independence. Politics acquired a halo of sacrifice and it gained the status of a religious activity. He injected economic, spiritual and social elements into politics which in the process became highly enriched. In short, Gandhi raised politics from the level of preoccupation to one of passion. The western dress of the politician disappeared, and khadi-woven Indian dress took its place. A congressman's dress consisted of khadi-woven *dhoti*, *kurta* and *cap*. It may thus be noted that the broad format of a typical politician was designed around this period of the nationalist movement in India. He evolved a high standard of conduct for the politician, and himself set the example before his followers by his practice of the high norms. Many devoted themselves exclusively to politics, the latter having become the mission of their life. But the full-time politician did not generally pose any problem either to himself or to the larger society. Persons from elitist background were coming to politics and even while becoming full-time politicians they had their independent means of living. At any rate, typical Indian family being a joint one was accustomed to absorbing one or two odd members and a full-time politician did not, therefore, appear to be a very astonishing or novel phenomenon in Indian society. Besides, life at that time was simple and wants were limited, and thus a full time political functionary did not impose any big economic burden either. Above all, the employment market itself was very limited and for many the only alternative to politics was some kind of a meaningless humdrum existence. Secondly, it became somewhat customary on the part of the Indian industrialists to extend a measure of financial support to politics and politicians. This indeed flows from a long standing Indian tradition wherein the wealthy people are expected to support noble activities and saintly personalities. The cause for which the politicians worked was patriotic and the key note of their living being on simplicity and austerity, politics was viewed as a saintly pursuit worthy of patronage by the society. The Birlas were for instance supporting Mahatma Gandhi, and that was the case with some other industrialists too. There were of course a few who were receiving some financial assistance from the parties, but their number was necessarily limited.

Independence and politician

An entry into politics was thus open ended during the period of national struggle for independence : its doors were open to any one prepared to make sacrifices. Independence of the country (1947) released new forces and pressures which in their turn made politics attract persons of altogether different orientation : politics became a power game having become election borne under the constitution ; politics has, indeed, come to seek its very legitimacy from elections. The politician in independent India starts his career, so to say, with a statement of lie : much more is his election expenditure than decreed under the law. This happened even with the first general election held in 1952, and the gap between the expenses incurred and legally allowed has been becoming increasingly more conspicuous over the years.

Electioneering is very expensive as it is governed by its own logic. The electoral constituency in India is very large, and a candidate has necessarily to tour its various parts, some even more than once. His campaigners are also required to undertake extensive tours in order to reach the people and canvass for him. He needs a battery of jeeps and other vehicles to ensure access to different parts of the constituency. With the rising price of petrol touring is necessarily very costly. He needs campaigners and workers, and they, too, have to be generally compensated. Publicity material is to be brought out, which again involves considerable expenditure. Funds are also to be spent on certain sections of voters these days. All taken together, it is extremely expensive to fight an election, and the election cost is getting pushed up by an over-riding desire on the part of every contestant to spend more than his rivals in the field. Of this expenditure only a part comes from the party, and the remainder is to be arranged by the candidate himself. Successive elections were becoming increasingly expensive and more fiercely contested. An average politician who comes from a rather humble origin with no inherited wealth is therefore obliged to mobilise the necessary resources to fight it. Politics becomes a career for him and a little taste of it revealed that it was an exceptionally lucrative even if a little insecure career. He, therefore, looks for persons who could provide the finances and organise campaign for him. The adoption of planning and of mixed economy pattern of development meanwhile expanded greatly the patronage of the state, and the businessmen, actual or required aspiring, the politician to help him in getting licences, permits, quotas or other benefits from the government of the day. He had also to reward his followers and workers. The politician, even if he could not become a minister, acted as an intermediary helping the businessman in his relationships with the government. Politics, thus, was becoming linkage politics.

Nor was the voter unchanging in his orientation. One who could ensure a block of votes acquired a bargaining power vis-a-vis the candidates and himself sought suitable compensation. It did not take long for money to flow freely in the constituency at the time of election. This in course of time made the elections even more expensive and further deepened his dependence on the money bags.

In short, electoral politics was beginning to produce its own logic and it became the seed-bed of corruption involving the politician, the fund-givers and even the voters. Politics has been fast becoming amoral, if not immoral also at times. This kind of the situation had emerged by the late sixties when the atmosphere became thick with talks about corruption in politics and administration. The commissions of inquiry set up against two politicians, one being a state chief minister and other a central minister, served to confirm the existence of widespread corruption in the public life of the country. What was novel about this phenomenon was its linkage with 'linkage politics' and its fast growing dimensions.

It is the Congress Party which shapes and controls the country's politics, and this party itself was undergoing a fundamental change in its internal composition. Each election brought in new elements. The split of 1969 was however the first major deliberately planned attempt at party renewal by recruiting, in one sweep, new elements having weak social commitments.

The process initiated with the first split received a big push when it suffered a second split in 1978. The pattern of electoral politics was also undergoing a change. It was becoming increasingly crude and the rules of the game were getting unashamedly molested. The periodic elections held on the basis of adult franchise were revolutionising politics, but the effects of the franchise power began to be felt most conspicuously after the fourth general election (1966-67). Malpractices such as rigging of election, booth-capturing, intimidation and electoral violence began to characterise the elections in many parts of the country. In short, in addition to money power, the muscle power also became a component of the emerging political culture of India. But the musclemen were content to operate from behind the scene. The linkage phenomenon was getting reinforced and lengthened, and politics was becoming medievialised, in the limited sense that it began to correspond with, and even accentuate, the existing social cleavages and habits of mind. The 'Eastminster' politician was evidently in the making.

In the early seventies the youth wing of the ruling Congress Party began to become more vocal and assertive and new elements were recruited into it. It is widely rumoured that many anti-social elements got into it to give a certain respectability to themselves and to insulate themselves from the arms of the law. It did not take long for such elements to graduate into the ruling party and occupy strategic positions. The second split in the Congress in the year 1978 gave a new and extended opportunity to such elements to gatecrash into the Congress (I) party and build it on the basis of skills possessed by them. But a crash programme of political recruitment took place in 1980 when first the Lok Sabha and later Assembly elections took place, finally leading to the emergence of the 'Eastminster' politician. While a number of musclemen have entered the legislatures many are operating from behind the scene. The complexion of the Congress Party, in short, has changed so much that there is a complete watershed between the old and the new. This is not to suggest that other parties have stayed completely untinged. The fact is that today almost all political parties in India are witnessing the induction of members with weak social commitments though, for obvious reasons, the ruling party being the corridor of power is apt to attract the undesirable elements more. It is no less revealing that the Janata-dominated state assembly of Uttar Pradesh in 1977 had out of a total membership of over 420 nearly eighty members who had the dubious credit of being 'history sheeters' according to the police records ; the number has gone over ninety in the Congress (I) dominated assembly elected in 1980. Bihar's assembly of 1980 includes nearly fifty persons who have been in the 'wanted' list of the police. All politicians seem to look so much alike ! The interface between politics and crime has in all likelihood come to stay in India, atleast in the foreseeable future.

The profile of the politician has thus been changing, so much so that the first generation politician would not be able even to recognise his contemporary successors and would, moreover, feel uneasy in the latter's company ! Even the second generation politician raised by Mahatma Gandhi would find apparently nothing in common between him and the modern politician the only thing shared by the two is perhaps the dress, or to be more correct, its yarn. The present day politician is not a continuation of the generation of path-makers nor of the generation of freedom-fighters. Indeed, he plainly marks discontinuity rather than continuity with the past.

But what of the society which has produced him and even perpetuates him ? The fact is that the Indian society itself has been witnessing a massive shift in its value system, orientations and attitudes. The developmental processes initiated under the five year plans and the pattern of politics in operation have totally weaned it away from its traditional anchorage, and in the process it has become aggressively materialistic in its outlook. What is more, the means to achieve results have become growingly irrelevant and irreverent in India and what is viewed as important is success, in the sense of amassing wealth and exhibiting it in vulgar consumerism. Selfishness today, stalks the land. The prevalent motto appears to be plainly and unashamedly 'self before society.' Values and graces of life have all but disappeared. Laws of the land are getting increasingly violated with impunity, especially by those who constitute the power-structure or have access to it. The society is afflicted with a deep crisis of character of such menancing magnitude that honesty has come very close to becoming a matter of opportunities. Amorality has verily become a way of life in the India of today. There is no organised citizen power or public opinion upholding the higher values of life. In short, the society itself has become corrupt, sick, baseless and normless. And, now it is the corrupt society which is getting reproduced in politics and professions, in public and private administration, indeed, in most areas of life. Nearly all professions and occupations in India are sickly. What is generally the operationally effective value system and professional norms of a doctor, a lawyer, a civil servant, a teacher, a contractor ?

An income-tax consultant, when asked by his client to show in the company account the funeral expenses of his recently dead father, quietly discovered the suitable sub-head to this purpose—'packaging and forwarding' !

The regulatory mechanisms of the past have become inoperative in modern India. Religion had in the past regulated to an extent the societal behaviour, but the way secularism has been interpreted in India has removed the fear of God from the minds of most, and a larger part of the society has a very faint ethical sensitivity. India, it seems, retired religion rather too prematurely—much before a secular value system could emerge and be assimilated. The politician is but a reminder, even though somewhat crude, of the state of health of the Indian society as a whole for which the style of democracy and development practised in the country are originally responsible but which, having reversed the role, is now producing its own images.

3

THE PARLIAMENTARIAN

THIS STUDY is based on interviews with a sample of fifty members of the Lok Sabha in late 1974 and early 1975. It shows that a high proportion of the problems brought to MPs by constituents are individual in nature rather than community-wide, including particularly requests for assistance in getting public and private jobs and preferential treatment within the civil service. Most MPs report that a majority of the problems raised by constituents actually come within the jurisdiction of the state rather than the Central government. Most MPs believe that they ought to try to meet individual constituent needs. They report that success in doing so depends heavily on informal techniques, developing contacts with both ministers and civil servants and with officials of the state governments. The conscientious MP faces a number of difficulties, involving both geographic distances and the allocation of time, in trying to maintain close linkages with his constituents.

INDIAN PARLIAMENT

In a parliamentary democracy such as India, the role and place of Parliament is of central importance both in ordering the affairs of the state and in shaping the larger social structures and processes. The Indian Parliament is bicameral, but it is the lower house, the Lok Sabha, that is the repository of power and authority. Hence, the focus of attention in the present chapter is on the Lok Sabha.

Currently, the Lok Sabha has a membership of 523 (excluding the speaker) ; each member is elected by the people on the basis of adult franchise. The membership is elected for a period of five years, unless dissolved earlier. The party positions at the beginning of 1975 are listed in Table 3.1.

Of the 523 members, 25 are women. The members of scheduled caste and scheduled tribe members are 77 and 41 respectively. Members of Parliament are also members of parliamentary committees (both standing and joint select committees). There are also informal consultative committees of MPs attached to each ministry of the central government ; an MP serves on two of his choice.

The Lok Sabha meets three times a year. The budget session begins in the middle of February and concludes in the middle of May. The monsoon session and the winter session last from the middle of July until the end of August and from the middle of November until the end of December, respectively. In 1974 it met for a total of 122 days (it does not normally meet on Saturdays and Sundays).

TABLE 3.1 : **Party membership in the Lok Sabha, 1975**

Name of Party	*Number of MPs*
Congress Party	357
Communist Party of India (Marxist) (CPI-M)	26
Communist Party of India (CPI)	24
Jana Sangh	20
Dravida Munnetra Kazhagam	19
Congress (Organisation)	12
Bhartiya Lok Dal	11
United Independent Parliamentary Group	11
Socialist Party	5
Anna Dravida Munnetra Kazhagam	5
Revolutionary Socialist Party	3
Kerala Congress	2
Muslim League	3
Forward Block	3
Telengana Praja Samiti	2
Unattached (Independent Members)	13
Vacant seats (to be filled by by-elections)	7
Total	523

A member of Parliament represents a population of over 8,00,000, organized in a territorial constituency. He is provided with an official residence in Delhi for which he is charged a moderate rent. He is paid a salary of Rs. 500 per month and, when the Lok Sabha is in session or when he is on parliamentary duty, he receives a daily allowance of Rs. 51. He is entitled to a first class railway pass with which he can travel throughout the country without any payment. The estimate of expenditures on MPs for the financial year 1974-75 is as follows ; salaries Rs. 2.9 million, and travel expenses, Rs. 10.1 million. The total expenditure on the Lok Sabha amounts to Rs. 31 million a year.

Methodology of study and profile of the sample

The present chapter is based on a study of a sample 50 members of Parliament, all drawn from the Lok Sabha. The sample taken is purposive in character : it is representative, as far as possible, of the diversities and varieties that the national legislature so vividly embodies and so eloquently expresses. Out of the total of 50 MPs interviewed by the author, 30 belonged to the ruling Congress Party (Table 3.2).

TABLE 3.2 : **Party Affiliation of Respondents**

Name of Party	*Number of MPs*
Congress Party	30
Bhartiya Lok Dal	4
CPI	1
CPI (M)	1
Dravida Munnetra Kazhagam	1
Jana Sangh	3
United Independent Parliamentary Group	1
Muslim League	1
Praja-Socialist Party	1
Revolutionary Socialist Party	1
Socialist Party	2
Independents	4
Total	50

According to the Census Report of 1971, 80 per cent of India's population is rural and the remaining 20 per cent dwells in cities and towns. This percentage is broadly reflected in the sample as well, with 38 of the respondents from rural and the remaining 12 from urban constituencies. Five of the 50 respondents were female. Seven respondents were in their 30s, 10 in their 40s, 21 in their 50s, and 12 were 60 or over.

A notable feuture of the Indian Constitution is the reservation of seats in the legislatures (as well as in the civil service) for members of what are called the scheduled castes and scheduled tribes. In the sample, 6 belong to scheduled castes and 4 to scheduled tribes, with the remaining 41 in the general category.

Each member of Parliament was interviewed by the author with the help of a questionnaire ; assurances were given that the interview was to be absolutely confidential with complete protection of the MP's identity. The interviews were conducted in November and December of 1974, and in January, March, April, and May of 1975.

Members of the public were not interviewed. The present study thus is based purely on the self-portraits of the parliamentary politicians. What the constituents think of their elected representatives on constiuency matters is out of the purview, although such a study should be enlightening.

Face of politics : Full-time or part-time

Members of Parliament may be said to fall into two broad occupational categories. Some combine parliamentary work with other professional involvment such as law, business, industry, farming, etc., thus regarding their parliamentary career as part-time ; others are full-time politicians, engaging in no other calling except politics. In the present sample, 40 MPs have politics as their occupation or pursuit, leaving only 10 in either business or a profession. Many respondents emphasized that the cadre-based parties, such as the CPI, CPI (M), and even the Jana Sangh, rigorously insist upon full-time parliamentarians. The full-time MPs argue that currently the parliamentary work load is heavy and entails so much preparation and responsibility that it demands a person's undivided attention. They also do not consider it very wholesome for an MP to engage in any money-earning activities while active in politics. "Farming is my occupation, but I am a full-time politician. I live a simple life and don't have to take up another occupation. It is not very salutary for an MP to take up some business. This is bound to interfere with his political and parliamentary life." Another commented : "Politics is a whole-time job and if one takes up any other work, the parliamentary activity is prone to get sacrificed ; moreover, one's thinking, too, may on occasion be influenced by commercial interest." On the other hand, the parliamentary members engaged in business greatly prize the independence that it confers on them. "One's own personality develops in an independent manner. Economic independence makes one more independent-minded. What can be worse than economic dependence which erases an MP's personality" ?

But politics has proved to be too jealous a mistress to let its devotees pursue other professions for long ; it tends to become an all-absorbing passion. Thus, although many MPs were initially part-time politicians, it did not take them long to discover that two swords could not lie in one scabbard. "In 1967 when I first entered the Lok Sabha," observed a parliamentarian, "I was devoting 60 per cent of my time to my professional work. It gradually diminished to 3 per cent, the big change occuring when I was elected president of my party." A journalist-parliamentarian similarly pointed out : "Since

1971, the year of my entry into the Lok Sabha, I have given up my profession of journalism. It is extremely difficult to combine any profession with politics, more so if one is anxious to become politically active. The really active element both in the Congress Party and in the opposition has no other profession as its master. The pressures of the constituency as well as of politics are constantly mounting, demanding a full-time parliamentarian."

In India, law and politics have gone together rather admirably. Such a combination dates back to the days of the British raj. The single largest professional group in the top political leadership of the country during the days of the national struggle for independence were lawyers The number of lawyers has always been large in Indian legislative chambers, both Central and state. In the present sample, 9 members (18%) have been in the legal profession. When asked about the relationship between law and parliamentary work, one lawyer-parliamentarian remarked :

> Parliament is a legislative chamber and people possessing a legal background have a very substantial contribution to make in legislative business. My legal background has given me an incisive attitude of analysing the issues and the problems that come before parliament. The qualities which make an effective lawyer are also the ones which make an effective parliamentarian : a man good at the bar is also good in parliament. Also, law gives one an independent base...he will not starve !

Constituency residence and allocation of time

The constituency linkage of a parliamentary politician cannot be fully understood without first obtaining an idea about his place of habitation. From this perspective, the MPs fall into two categories : those who have their residence in the constituency and those who reside outside it. The electoral laws of India are explicit that a candidate for the state legislature must be "an elector (i.e. a registered voter) for any assembly constituency in that state", a person to be chosen for Lok Sabha must be "an elector for any parliamentary constituency", and a candidate for the Rajya Sabha (upper house of Indian Parliament) must be "an elector for a parliamentary constituency in that state"[1] (emphasis added). This means that while a state legislator and a member of Rajya Sabha must be a resident of that

1. Quotations are from the Representation of the People Act, 1951, Sections 6, 4 and 3.

state, an aspirant for the Lok Sabha may seek election from any constituency in the country.

In the sample of 50, 21 parliamentarians (42 per cent) do not have their normal dwellings within the constituency. Of this number, 14 belonged to the Congress Party, two each to Jana Sangh and Bhartiya Lok Dal, and one each to CPI (M) and Muslim League, and one was Independent. The non-resident members, especially the opposition members, have generally been both prominent leaders of their respective parties and well-known personalities in the country. Most, however, do belong to the state in which their constituency lies. Such members must necessarily divide their time between New Delhi, where the Lok Sabha sits, and the constituency. Those reporting 40 days a year or less in the constituency have all been non-residents. On the face of it, their contacts with the constituency are bound to be less intimate, notwithstanding the assertion of an MP that "it is in Delhi that one has to exert his influence if the constituency is to be benefited, it is an extraodinarily centralized administration today."

But the reverse position is not necessarily a consolation, much less a boon to the constituents. An MP staying in the constituency may technically spend a longer period in it but he may stir out of his house only occasionally, thus affording little jubilation to the citizens. The crucial test is touring the villages and more remote areas, meeting all categories of people, discussing their problems, and taking organized steps to solve them. This is an organizational problem, and here the role of the political party also becomes significant. An MP put this problem trenchantly :

> Six months in a year are rainy in Eastern India. My constituency has 80 per cent rural areas. One cannot move in a rural area during the rainy season nor during the period of 'loo' (that is, intense heat). If an MP can spend two months in his constituency, he should indeed be a lucky man. Going to a constituency does not necessarily mean that an MP is effective in his constituency ; a detailed programme must be prepared well in advance of the visit and widely publicized, too. Many MPs confine themselves to the district headquarters ; they meet the district collector, manipulate publicity in the local press, and that's all. Without a network of workers and prior publicity, touring is not very fruitful.

Moreover, touring has been adversely affected by an unprecedented rise in the price of gasoline.

It should be interesting to know the amount of time the parliamentarians spend in their constituencies. Half of the MPs in the sample report spending 41 to 80 days a year in the constituency. Of the two MPs reporting "161 days and above," one represents the parliamentary constituency of Delhi ; the other was previously a state legislator and also a state-level minister, and his reply indicates where his heart truly lies. He commented :

> I was much more effective—and happy—when I was an MLA. The ordinary citizen has problems which demand state action, not central action. As an MP, I can't give as much time to my constituency as I did when I was a state legislator. The population of my constituency is nearly 10 lakhs and it is a sprawling one. The central government is a remote entity so far as the problems of the ordinary citizens are concerned.

TABLE 3.3 : **Time spent by MPs in constituencies**

Number of days per year Spent in Constituency	*Number of MPs*
0-40	10
41-80	25
81-120	11
121-160	2
161-and above	2
Total	50

Categories of problems presented to MPs

One way of classifying the problems brought to the MPs could be whether they are of an individual nature or are of general community-wide interest. A request for the MPs help in the matter of employment for someone would be classified as a personal matter, while a demand for a school, road, railway station, or post office may be considered to be of general interest. The present study discloses that an overwhelmingly large portion of an MP's agenda is made up of individual requests from his constituents (Table 3.4). It is not uncommon for a people perennially haunted by poverty, hunger, and employment to remain more concerned with their own individual problems. Only after the basic physical needs of a people are moderately satisfied do they venture into articulating demands of a more general, community-wide interest. The present very low constituent concern for community-wide needs can also be noted in Table 3.4.

TABLE 3.4 : **Proportion of total problems brought to MPs : Individual and general**

Percentage of Total Problems that are Individual	*Number of MPs*	*Percentage of Total Problems that are General*	*Number of MPs*
Up to 50	3	0-10	24
51-60	3	11-20	12
61-70	4	21-30	10
71-80	12	31-40	2
81-90	26	41-50	1
91-100	2	51 and above	1
Total	50	Total	50

Individual problems

The variety of individual problems is immense—and has sometimes a rather disturbing effect on the mind of the listener. Most of them, however, could be put into the following categories :

(1) employment ;
(2) harassment by police and revenue officials ;
(3) civil service matters ;
(4) Land disputes (in rural constituencies) ;
(5) agricultural inputs—water, seeds, fertilizers, credtit (also rural) ;
(6) civil supplies such as foodgrains, coal, cooking oil ;
(7) certificates of character and residence ;
(8) admission to educational institutions, particularly medical, engineering, and technical, during the opening sessions.

In the metropolitan cities like Calcutta and Delhi, a very large number of people approach their MPs for the allotment of houses or for stopping demolition of slums where they live. Interestingly, the cases of harassment by police have been reported to be much lower in sophisticated localities of a city such as Delhi : "In this constituency the police are more well behaved, as the people living in this area are well-to-do, educated, and quite articulate." Another parliamentary politician made a similar claim, albeit in a different context : "My presence has been sensed by the local officials. They behave towards the people in a civil way because they know that I am the MP from this area." The police "zulum" (atrocity), however, is a more common experience in the rural areas. In the industrialised areas MP's also are confronted by problems presented by businessmen, such as licences, quotas of raw materials, transportation, financial assistance, and restrictions on imports and exports.

To wealthy MPs, the constituents ask particularly for employment and even outright monetary assistance. That none but the rich MPs have mentioned people approaching them for financial help indicates that the people have a sense of where the purse is located. An MP belonging to the former princely family expressed her dilemma thus :

> I don't have the advantage of other MPs : I can't mix and mingle with the people in the same way as others do. If I begin doing this, it is apt to be resented by my people. My people look to me with reverence and respect. The largest number of people coming to me ask for monetary assistance. I owe it to my ancestors and to my people to help the needy—the old persons, the widows, the destitute, the poor having marriageable daughters. No rich person comes to me ; they don't need me. The rich and the *nouveau riche* make money out of the government, and they are completely outside my orbit.

A few MPs interviewed have been active in the trade unions of government personnel. Indeed, the lower grade government employees, who are fairly organised in India, constitute the stronghold and dependable source of political power and status of these MPs. They get the largest number of requests from this highly vociferous group in India. These mainly relate to such problems as non-implementation of government orders relating to service matters of the employees, supersession of employees, disciplinary action, and demands relating to wages and service conditions.

To the MPs of the ruling party—and only of the ruling party—requests for state patronage come in large numbers. Men and women flock to them for membership on government committees, commissions, and foreign delegations, for national awards, and for other ornamental or sinecure offices. It should be mentioned that such approaches are made only to those parliamentarians of the ruling party who have earned a reputation of being very close to the political chief executive. One such MP confided :

> This year alone, I faced 200 persons who wanted my recommendation for the award for padma-sri.

Another MP known for her connections with the "establishment" observed ;

> I get another set of politically ambitious ladies aspiring for memberships and awards—membership of committees and delegations and award of padma-sri : 60 per cent of them are educated and 40 per cent are 'politically' educated.

One may wonder at the absence in the above list of cases of corruption involving the civil service. In a way corruption is implied in item two above (harassment by police and revenue officials). Although no great public fuss about corruption involving civil servants is raised, this should not suggest that it does not exist or that it is presently under firm political and administrative control ; such corruption in the civil service does exist, but recently it has been accepted by the citizens as but a normal pattern of life in modern India. As an MP put it candidly:

> Corruption is now regarded as but a part of life. If by greasing an official's palms the work gets done, it is no longer a grievance as such. But if even after bribery nothing gets done, it becomes a grievance. The safest money-lending, today, is to a civil servant, especially to a would be police constable.

In a country where unemployment stares at almost every other young face, the pressure for jobs is intense and incessant. There is also a nearly universal belief that without "shifarsh" (recommendation) it is practically impossible to get a job ; a Member of Parliament is consequently flooded with requests for such recommendations. The pressure is much heavier for the parliamentarians of the ruling political party. The ruling party has obviously greater power of patronage, although much depends on the personality of the member too.

Every respondent observed that civil service matters like postings, transfers, and promotions of public personnel came to them in ample profusion. Most respondents (and notably, all the MPs of the ruling party) put their number at a figure only slightly less than that for jobs. A ruling party MP from a state capital reported the single largest number of requests as falling in this category. It may be more expressive to let an MP speak on this aspect.

> The service matters—transfers, postings, promotions, etc.—brought to me are second only to the cases for jobs. Among the callers, the personnel of class III and IV (i.e., clerical and lower staff) are predominant but even some class II and I civil servants

> also come. The government servants approach me either directly or their parents come. The largest number of cases are for postings in or nearer the home town. Some people get superseded when promotions are made and they come to me for redress of grievances.

Another commented ;

> The civil servants who come to me range from the district magistrate right down to the 'chaprasi' (peons). Indeed, Class I officers have been putting pressure on me more than the lower class personnel.

An overwhelmingly large proportion of the service matters concern the state government and are brought by state government employees. Central government personnel are concentrated in the railways, posts and telegraphs, and defence, and only to a slightly less extent in excise and customs. Since the nationalisation of leading banks in 1969, matters relating to the banking institutions too have begun to come to the MPs. The personnel of a central ministry are also reported to be coming to an MP who is a member of the Informal Consultative Committee attached to that ministry. The largest number of cases relating to the Central Government, however, come from the railways.

Community problems

As indicated, the other category of problems brought to MPs by the constituents are issues of general, community-wide interest. Almost without exception, such matters are brought by people in groups, the panchayati raj leadership or influential persons of an area. Such groups of people articulate the development needs of the locality, which include opening railway lines and railway stations including mail trains, providing post and telegraph offices, schools, clinics, roads, rural electrifications, increased irrigational facilities, and agricultural credit. Since the country is vast and diversified no standard, universal and yet comprehensive inventory of community problems can be compiled.

While individual problems are brought by both the poor and the wealthy, the needs of the community and the locality are articulated by the relatively well-to-do, the influential, and the politically conscious groups in the constituency, acting in accordance with the parameters of their own value-system. This is the unanimous verdict of the data collected in the present study. The impulse of development has yet to touch the poorest in the community ; the latter have not yet been permeated by the developmental ethos nor have been attracted towards the nation-building programmes of the government. Even more pathetic, a large number of MPs confided that the really indigent and the down-trodden do not really come. "The poorest are resigned to their fate ; they are the most uncomplaining of all."

MPs AND STATE GOVERNMENT

The range and volume of matters brought to the MPs is impressive ; even more striking, the constitutional boundaries drawn between the national and the state legislators are largely ignored. Since India is a federal state, there is a constitutional division of functions between the Centre and the constituent units called states. Under this system, the MP's direct concern is only with those functions belonging to the Central government. Subjects like law and order, police, agriculture, irrigation, electricity, education, cooperatives, small scale industries, and public health come under the direct control of the state government and as such come within the direct responsibility of the state legislators.[2] However, constituents, particularly in the rural areas, do not comprehend such functional differentiation. Therefore, they bring to their MP not only problems and matters that are the centre's direct concern but also those that fall within the state's field. Twenty-three of the 50 respondents reported that over 80 per cent of the problems brought to them by constituents fell within the jurisdiction of the states, and another 20 reported that more than 60 per cent of the problems were in that category. Thus, although an MP's constitutionally specified role is limited to the central sphere of functions, his major workload coming from his constituents related to the state's field. The single respondent who reported that only 10 per cent of the total volume of the problems related to the state's field said :

> I don't have influence with the state government although it is may party which is in power. My constituents, too, have come to realize this.

It is true that some citizens approach both the MP and the state legislator simultaneously for the same problem in an effort to

2. Although electricity has been placed in the concurrent list in the Constitution, it is the immediate responsibility of the state.

reinforce their case, or perhaps to ensure that at least one of the two will help ; yet this does not alter the significance of the above data. It therefore follows that the parliamentary politicians must remain in close and continuous contact both with their state governments and with the MLAs of their constituencies to facilitate the smooth and quick fulfilment of citizen demands.

Quite often both MPs and MLAs belong to the same political party, the Congress, which would seemingly ease their task. However, a party may be bedeviled by internal factionalism. This is certainly true of the ruling Congress Party, which is heterogeneous and includes many former members of other parties. If the MPs and the MLAs formally belong to the same political party but happen to be in different factions, they may not function as a team, thereby making their coordinated efforts difficult, if not altogether impossible. Even if such a division does not exist, their working styles may differ, making any enduring collaboration between them practically impossible. Opposition MPs have complained of a nearly complete lack of cooperation and coordination between them and the state legislators belonging to a different political party. They assume that problems of cooperation would disappear if the MLA belonged to the same party, but the experience of the Congress MPs certainly does not appear to justify such thinking.

Even at the best of times, an MP is thus seen to engage in performing functions of an MLA without, of course, sitting in the state legislature and doing legislative work. The MLA's role devolves upon him completely, in a sense even formally, when his state happens to be brought under presidential rule under Article 356 of the Constitution. This at once adds considerably to the volume, range, and intensity of his participation in the affairs of his state. Under such circumstances, his constituency role becomes direct and unshared and his contact with the state government more frequent. With the state legislators gone, his ombudsmanic role becomes more prominent. One MP in the present sample had his state government as well as the urban government of his constituency superseded. Under such political compulsions, he discovered himself functioning simultaneously as an MP, an MLA, and a municipal corporator.

It is necessary here to note that not all these problems are necessarily brought to all the MPs. People do tend to assess their MPs and adjust their behaviour accordingly. Their representatives, too, seem to have realized this broad truth. "If the people get an impression that an MP is active and politically influential, the number of his visitors increases—and so do their demands," an MP observed.

In addition to constituent demands, an MP is also mobilised for the purpose of promoting the interests of his state at the level of the central government. This propensity is much more marked in the case of those who belong to the party currently in power in their state. A chief minister makes a special point to maintain a liasion with the MPs from his state and to use them as a lobby for its demands at the centre (as well as for his career advancement if he belongs to the Congress). The Congress in particular, has approached this task in a more organised way. It has its committees of MPs for each state, who remain in contact with their respective state governments ; the effectiveness of this mechanism of course depends upon the political stature of the chief minister, his rapport with the central ministers from his state and his own MPs, and finally and very inportantly, his relationship with the prime minister.

INTERMEDIARIES

All the MPs in the present sample report that, although many people approach them independently, some are accompanied by political workers who are known to the MPs or, at any rate, who pretend to have known them and whose purpose is to enlist their support in the matter. The number of these intermediaries recently has been increasing. While many of them are activated by a desire to help and also to carve out for themselves a place of influence and respect in the local community, this practice is not entirely without risk and abuse.

The intermediaries initiate a process that tends to insulate the representative from the citizens : they interpose themselves, thereby increasing the distance between the two. In the course of time the MP is prone to look at the constituency problems in a highly filtered, selective way through the eyes of those intermediaries. Dependence on them is seen to be much more marked in the case of those MPs who do not live in the constituency they represent. Unfortunately, some of the intermediaries are nothing short of political touts. One MP, having vast experience in politics and a reputation for integrity and a sense of dedication, commented rather philosphically :

> Power has itself become a vested interest in India. At various levels of political life right from the secretariat to the village levels, there has been spawned a class of brokers or procurers, go-betweens between the citizens and the wielders of power. As power has remained with the Congress Party all these years, it

has attracted to itself all kinds of unsavoury persons. A parasitic class has emerged in India particularly in the Congress. The United Front Government in the state of—in which we, too, were a partner gave me an experience of these self-seekers and sycophants. The gate of every district town hospital has 'agents' connected with the doctors ; the doctors have connections with nursing homes. Indeed, it is, today, a scramble among the mercenaries. No one can insulate himself from the onslaughts of such agents, much less the political parties, much less the Congress.

Other Methods of Contact

Besides visiting and touring his constituency, there are other methods by which the MP may remain in touch with the constituents. The constituents may themselves visit Delhi and present their problems to the MP. This approach is generally used by those who live near Delhi and by the more articulate and well-to-do constituents. The constituents may also write to him appraising him of their problems and soliciting his intervention. Of the 46 respondents who were able to make an estimate, 11 received no more than 100 letters a month, 17 received from 101 to 500, and 18 received more than 500 (up to a maximum of 6,000).

The bulk of the mail includes mimeographed material sent by various organizations as part of their publicity programme ; these groups are not necessarily from an MP's constituency. The material continues to flow to him from organized groups that want to make their views known to the law-makers. The rest of the mail includes letters from the constituency, from the state, and from the country a whole, depending upon his own political stature in the land. Although MPs receive correspondence from strangers, most flows from persons acquainted with the MP, including party workers, the more vocal groups in the constituency, and citizens who are victims of the "insolence of authority" and who, therefore, look to him for redress of their grievances. His mail bag also includes communications that are in the nature of reminders, drawing attention to a previously discussed matter that the MP had promised to pursue. Usually these letters seek personal favours.

A few MPs scrupulously acknowledge every letter that is received. "Invariably, every letter coming to me is answered. This, I have found from my experience, has a powerful impact on the constituents. People take my letter around and show it to others. This builds up my image in the constituency." But acknowledgement and reply do not appear to be the regular practice of most MPs. The following two observations seem to be characteristic : "I reply to letters worth replying to" ; "I do the work mentioned in the letter, but don't get time to reply." It should be mentioned here that the legislators in India receive no stenographic or office assistance from the state. A third method by which the constituents may contact the MP is by the gradual introduction of subscriber trunk telephone dialling system. As might be anticipated, this is a device helpful only to the affluent sections in bigger cities.

Although not widely invoked in practice, yet another method is that of popular agitation, which, among other goals, seeks to enlist constituency loyalty. One MP in the sample uses this device very much like the proverbial stone to kill two birds. "Every year we (referring to his party) offer one satyagraha (agitation) in our constituency, court arrest and spend seven to ten days in the jail, where we organise a training camp for our workers--a truly nationalized training camp at that ! "

MPs' response to constituent requests

The reader may be curious to know about the MPs' manner of dealing with such a wide assortment of problems. How do MPs react to the request of their constituents ? What is the modus operandi of the MPs ? In response to question asking if MPs should entertain individual requests from their constituents or confine themselves to the community problems alone, the views of the 50 MPs interviewed are divided ; 12 of them think that an MP ought not to involve himself in cases of individual concern, but should concentrate on general problems of his constituency, optimising his effectiveness as an elected leader of the people. As one stated :

> I do not believe in solving the individual problems : no single individual can take up this responsibility. Moreover, some of the individual problems are conflicting in nature.

These are the political aristocrats of the Indian parliamentary system. This may be the strait and narrow path of virtue, but in India's situation it does not lead to heaven. This is realised by all in the sense that even these 12 MPs do not in practice completely spurn individual cases of constituents. Only one MP observed that he did not entertain individual problems and concentrated exclusively on collective issues. "But an MP can resist involving himself in individual cases only at his own peril", commented a repondent ; and he was firm in his view that no parliamentary politician in India has ceased to take interest in the individual problems of the constituents. Where a large majority of population is living below and near the poverty line and where the traditions of government have been authoritarian, personal help from the elected representatives is actively sought. It is not without reason that the most cherished image of an eltcted representative in India is that of a helper and a sharer of people's personal joys, anxieties, even sorrows. From the point of view of citizens, an ideal MP must be an ombudsman for them.

The MPs' tactics

What do the MPs do about the problems and issues brought to them ? The MPs do not command executive authority in any field and at best enjoy only a recommendatory status. When they decide to take up a particular matter, either individual or collective, they write or speak to the ministers and/or civil servants concerned. An MP of long standing put the whole matter in this way :

> For larger community-wide issues, the forum of parliament needs to be used to create public opinion and to bring to bear upon the government the people's demands. For individual things one has to bring to bear one's own weight as an MP and as a public figure in the corridors of power, in the secretariat—even behind the back of ministers, if need be, and with their support and concurrence, if necessary.

A status of equality with the chief minister and other important state level ministers is among the requisites of a successful MP. He meets and writes to the members of the political executive of the state in connection with the problems of his constituency (as well as for political purposes). Most of them also meet or write to the state-level civil servants. Currently, an MP can scarcely avoid meeting functionaries like the district collector. the superintendent of police, even the block development officer. Indeed, he would neglect this only at his own peril ! A respondent observed :

> An MP has no effective power : he has to run to the district collector to get anything done. Moreover, the bureaucracy is so powerful that one has to handle it diplomatically : mere telephone talk is not enough.

The MPs make a large number of recommendations to ministers and officials for jobs, service matters, supplies and other things. It is interesting that a number of MPs make recommendations without meaning to recommend. "I have to listen to the visitors. I recommend the application in every case. Only in the case of a person who is really honest and well meaning do I speak privately to the officer concerned."

Only 4 MPs have reported, on grounds of principle, refusal to meet either ministers or civil servants—except, of course, on social occasions. Another 5 MPs believe in meeting only the ministers to discuss the constituents' problems ; they defend such an approach by arguing that it is inappropriate on the part of the elected representatives to deal directly with civil servants. Nearly four-fifths of the respondents meet both ministers and civil servants. As regards speaking over the telephone, nearly all of them do it, and do it on a rather lavish scale (they are provided telephones by the state).

The respondents' replies seem to lead to the following findings. In quite a wide range of issues, it is not the intrinsic merit of a case that ultimately matters, but the crucial factor is who espouses it. Not all MPs are treated alike, even by bureaucrats apparently socialised in Weberian traits. The stature of an MP and his political complexion are among the important inputs in determining the output.

Secondly, there is an astonishingly widespread belief among both the Congress and the opposition MPs about the general ineffectiveness of political executives as a class and the nearly decisive voice of the bureaucracy in the actual ordering of affairs in the land. Before a reader is treated to a few excerpts from the interviews he needs to be reminded that the code of conduct for legislators borbids discourses with civil servants for such matters ; they are expected to deal with the ministers :

> I do meet civil servants including the clerks. Sometime back, I found that what clerks did for me, even the ministers could not do. I began meeting the clerks after I discovered that even powerful ministers were ineffective in the face of opposition from the clerks in the secretariat.
>
> Bureaucracy is a permanent fixture in India. A minister who is in conflict with is secretary is liable to forfeit his office. Only those ministers have been successful who know the knack of carrying on with the civil servants. The bureaucrats rule India ; they know the politicians can do nothing without them.

> It is much easier to get things done by talking to the secretary or the joint secretary. Even if I meet the minister, he would pass the paper down to the secretary and the joint secretary for advice and action. The secretary and the joint secretary, when met, want to oblige and the work is done more expeditiously.
>
> I meet every one in administration including PAs (Personal Assistants) to ministers. It is easier to get things done by contacting the PA to the minister. The PAs feel immensely pleased when an MP goes to them and provide valuable clues for getting the work done. I find meeting the PA more fruitful than meeting the minister.
>
> The secretary (to the government) has a grasp of his subject and so can immediately make up his mind about the matter I take with me. Unless a particular thing goes against the announced policy decisions of the political executive, he can quickly take a decision. Most ministers don't know their jobs and would like to depend on their civil servants.
>
> I find the specialists more helpful in getting things done, especially in the developmental areas, than the generalist administrator.

Finally, because the country is perceived to be actually ruled by the civil servants, writing is considered by many to be more weighty than merely meeting and speaking to them ; one-third of the MPs observe the practice of a written communication following their meeting with the minister or the civil servants. One MP said :

> I meet the ministers in the Central Hall of Parliament. I prefer to write. A letter, being formal, has greater impact. The minister at least reads it and then it goes down to the bureaucratic levels. In India the bureaucracy is supreme ; so it is the paper that is effective.

Another one commented :

> I believe in writing letters to the ministers and the civil servants. In writing letters one is aware of one's sense of responsibility.

Reaction to Civil Service Matters

What is the reaction of the MPs to the civil service matters brought to them ? The lower grade public personnel show keen interest in the matter of their postings and transfers. As a rule, they seek posting in or near their home town or at a place of their choice. The general plea made is the old age of parents or their sickness and hence a desire to be near their bedside "in the evening of their life." A married couple seeks posting at the same station. Cases of transfers and postings are also brought by Class II and I civil servants but unaccompanied by such rationalisations. They seek postings in "good" departments and stations. As transfers become increasingly politically motivated, some of the affected civil servants even approach rival parties for help and intervention in the matter. If, as is generally the case, the harassment is caused by the ruling party, they go to the MP of the opposition party, taking at the same time every care that "they do not get noticed by the ruling party." Besides the cases of postings and transfers, those of supersession and disciplinary action also come to the MPs. The civil servants at higher levels of the government are reported to bring cases of promotion (in addition to postings in good departments and places).

Almost all opposition MPs and a few Congress MPs show a general reluctance to pursue these matters concerning individual civil servants, and relent only in cases of extreme hardship and prima facie injustice. To quote one such MP :

> Only on compassionate grounds do I interest myself in such matters of postings and transfers. People bring supersessions cases. If I am prima facie convinced that a case is genuine, I take it up. I don't take sides in such cases ; otherwise. I would be doing a wrong to a person But, as you know, there is sometimes arbitrariness in matters of promotions, and as a result of my writing, the wrong has been righted. I have also found that in cases where severe forms of penalty were imposed, the governmental action was just.

An extreme stance in this regard has been adopted by only one MP who observed :

> The civil servants are afraid to come to me. I am a socialist and don't care for them : they already have enough leverage and can easily get things done.

It is, however, the members of the ruling party who take up these cases in large numbers. The civil servants belonging to scheduled castes flock around the MPs of their community with requests. The following observation made by one of the MPs may be considered to be typical :

> I try to help them whenever possible. I telephone, meet, or write to the officers concerned. I also speak to the minister when I feel that such a step would be necessary. I particularly help those who help me. For instance, I helped the district magistrate because he had helped me in the past. Politics is not for the idealists, at any rate in India today.

When asked about the rate of his success in such forays he put the figure at 50 per cent, saying that when everyone who matters makes a recommendation, the recommendations are mutually cancelling ! Before this discussion is concluded it seems necessary to repeat that the civil service rules of the centre and of the states expressly forbid the civil servants from soliciting, directly or indirectly, help from elected representatives. However, in practice, no disciplinary action, as contemplated in these rules, is taken.

Members of Parliament and voluntary organisations

The MPs are also seen to figure in various organisations in the constituency. While membership of some may be ex-officio,[3] they also seek the membership of others or may even be requested to accept the membership. Each respondent was asked in what ways the membership of these bodies contributed to his effectiveness as a parliamentary politician ; 40 of them, including all the MPs of the ruling party, favoured the parliamentary politicians getting into these organisations. Membership in the various bodies in the constituency helps impart intimate knowledge of the problems of the continuency. The MP finds himself in a position to exercise a sobering influenee on the work of these bodies and thus prevent them from taking recourse to possible unhealthy methods. The membership also enables him to forge and consolidate his contacts with the various cross-sections of the people of his area. This, in turn, grants him independence from his political party in the constituency. It also strengthens his power vis-a-vis other political parties. In the eyes of the people as well as the government, he derives a special standing, which helps him in carrying out his responsibilities more efficiently. When all is said and done, such membership provides an MP with a base for power and influence, to be ultimately pressed into service

3. For instance, the zila parishad.

to win elections. This is what most of the respondents favouring the membership of these bodies have themselves conceded.

Ten of them, on the other hand, resist any such involvement. The arguments advanced by them are to stay out of the local politics, and a desire to enlist the "total" support of the constituency in their role as MPs and finally, non-availability of time. One MP puts it this way :

> I stay out of these bodies, although I know that the members of the . . . Party have captured most of these bodies. Politicians seek membership for exploitation, financial or political or both, as is common in post-Gandhi India.

Members of Parliament and constituency aursing

An MP's knowledge of his constituency and acquaintance with his constituents is generally not so deep as that of a member of the state legislative assembly. The constituency of the state legislator is much smaller, indeed it is one-sixth or one-seventh of the parliamentary constituency, and this fact alone requires at least seven fold (indeed, more) effort on the part of the Member of Parliament to maintain the same level of contact with his constituents. Secondly, the functions entrusted to the Central government under the constitution are such that they do not touch directly and immediately the lives of ordinary men and women. The MP is offered more opportunities to work with national and international themes. The problems agitating the minds of the people in the constituency do not as a rule fall within his direct parliamentary responsibility. Also, it is not physically possible for a Member of Parliament to spend as much time in his constituency as an MLA can do. Parliamentary sessions last for nearly seven months of the year, and an MP who is devoted to his parliamentary work must necessarily study the various problems very carefully and prepare himself adequately. He is also a member at least of a few parliamentary committees, which also require time and energy. Further, the MPs go abroad as members of parliamentary delegations when parliament is not in session. All these responsibilities leave an MP less time for his constituency and its immediate problems. This is particularly so in the case of MPs not rooted in the constituency. The activities in parliament necessarily receive publicity in the national press. In the process, MPs who are more active in the Parliament and its committees have more opportunities to become "national" figures, involving themselves in wider, national problems. While a constituency reads its MP's name in the press and (if it is an urban one) rejoices in the fact that he has attained a national stature, it also gets further removed from its elected representative.

This handicap tends to be less marked in the case of an MP who had earlier served as a state legislator. Six MPs in the present sample had done so, and they continue to spend more time in the constituency than others ; they evince more intimate knowledge of local conditions and are more people-oriented than issue-oriented. But the number of MPs who have functioned as state legislators is not very large in India. The political parties do not insist on previous state legislative experience as some kind of a precondition or qualification for party nominations to parliament. This indeed is part of the larger political culture of the country : local governmental experience is counted as having little relevance for party nominations of candidates for the state legislative assembly.

Ruling party and opposition MPs

It is necessary to consider, even if briefly and inconclusively, whether the effectiveness of the parliamentary politicians depends upon the party labels they wear. This is another way of asking : is membership of the ruling party seen to confer an obvious abvantage in meeting the constituency expectations ? The question may be dealt within two parts : central government and state government.

Until recently, most MPs of the opposition parties perceived no unfair discrimination in the treatment given to them by the central ministers and civil servants. One who has been an MP since Jawaharlal Nehru's days referred warmly to what he called the "Nehru tradition" of cordiality to all Members of Parliament regardless of their political affiliations. They concede that the members of the ruling party enjoy greater patronage, which they do not begrudge very much. The enormity of the problems transcends the formal boundaries between the various political parties. The political divisions, thus, find areas of overlap, and in the process are prevented from becoming totally and mutually exclusive. Besides, as another MP put it :

> Powerful opposition MPs command a nuisance value today. It is the vocal cord of a member which determines his capacity to get things done in the government. Not infrequently, the Congress MPs ask me to raise certain matters on the floor of the House. Even some ministers secretly send cases of victimisation and corruption to me with the request to raise them in the Lok Sabha.

These MPs, however fear an erosion of the "Nehru tradition," and point to a number of straws in the wind. In short, they tend to look to the future with a measure of uncertainty and anxiety.

What do the MPs of the ruling party think about themselves and the opposition MPs? Many admit that as a part of the "establishment" they do, and should, have an edge over their counterparts of the opposition parties. When asked to react to such a widely held view, one of them said rather excitedly:

> Effectiveness is an individual quality, not dependent on party affiliations. Coming to your question, I may say that an opposition MP often carries greater weight in the corridors of power. Many in the government are corrupt and are always afraid of public exposure. Hence the special effort to keep the opposition in good humour. We in the Congress have been reduced to mere digits now, just taken for granted.

With regard to their effectiveness in dealing with state government, the opposition MPs find themselves in an increasingly helpless position. Many have complained about a distinct partisan spirit overtaking the state governments, rendering opposition MPs "not very effective." As one put it:

> Since 1971 a partisan trend in the state government is discernible. There is political vicitimisation in the state. Even senior civil servants are afraid of doing anything for the opposition if they feel that the decision they are inclined to make might go against the wishes of their political chief.

This feeling of helplessness is contributing, in a certain measure, to the alienation of these MPs from the larger political values, institutions, and processes. This, to be sure, does not augur well for the continued functionality and vitality of the political system. It is not completely unlikely that the recent spurt in agitational politics and anomic phenomena in the country stems, at least partly, from this growing disillusionment with the parliamentary system.

Although only one of the several linkages that a Member of Parliament currently maintains, the constitutency linkage provides the base for the forging of others. Herein lies its uniqueness. While it does not lead to newspaper publicity and widespread recognition for the MP, this linkage is the one most cherished, at least by a large section of the population. Its richness would indeed be the song of the constituency heard long after its hero disappears from the scene. This should be no small consolation to those MPs who maintain such a linkage, even though in the process they may have to reduce their involvement in larger, headline-making themes.

CONCLUSIONS

The present study shows that persons nearly at the bottom of the economic ladder have had little contact with their legislators. They tend not to approach them, preferring rather to remain content with the lot which Providence has given them. Nor do the legislators seem to make any special effort to reach out to them. Such sections of the poor as have organised themselves and have demonstrated their political relevance may, and do, command their attention, particulary at the time of elections. Yet the politicians tend to remain surrounded by the articulate, the well-organised, or the well-to-do sections of the society, and generally the latter's eye is on possible benefits to be gained or extracted from the government. The voiceless citizens like old persons, widows, handicapped people, and the unorganised sections of the population remain outside the orbit of the politicians' attention.

Moreover, the odds confronting an MP are many and great. With nearly seven months to be spent in parliamentary work, he is left with only a few months to spend in his constituency. The parliamentary constituency covers a large geographical area ; its population also is quite large. These factors do not make it easy or even possible for a national legislator, however well-meaning he is, to forge and deepen his contacts with a very large share of his constituents. In this respect, the local political hierarchies could be of help both to poorer citizens and to the legislators. But these organisations themselves are usually controlled by persons having narrow political attitudes rather than wide humanist orientations, and those who view the poor as having little political significance.

The citizens, as the study discloses, remain almost completely immersed in their own individual problems, evincing a very low concern for issues of community-wide interest. While the poor are almost totally absorbed in matters affecting them individully, such as harassment by the police and the revenue officials, agricultural credits, or employment, and so on the relatively well-to-do—the "new rich" seek, in very large numbers, individual favours and benefits such as telephone connections for themselves and the like. The "felt needs" of the locality, however, come to be articulated by the upcoming richer classes and the influential and politically conscious groups residing there.

The legislators, too, on their part find the resultant closer contacts with such groups rewarding, both politically and otherwise. For, it is these groups and classes in the constituency that are capable of mobilising resources and support for them, without which successful election is impossible today. In the process, a relationship of reciprocity, of give and take, between the legislators and such groups is established. Development administration, particularly rural development, has come to acquire a fairly distinct class character in India, supported by a rather narrow social and economic base in the community.

This study confirms the existence and proliferation of points of direct contact between the politicians and the civil servants. Moreover, this relationship has evolved by the deliberate bypassing of both of the established hierarchies. This has come about because the hierarchies, both poltical and administrative, are perceived in effect to be counter-productive. The violation of hierarchical structure is seen to expedite decision making in many matters but it also makes possible corruption of micro-level politics. The net effect is that both the politician and the civil servant have learned by now to accomodate each other in a wide variety of matters. Taken together, it is an open-ended oligarchy that wields the levers of power in India.

Although parliamentary democracy postulates primacy of the politician over the bureaucracy, in realty it is the latter that continues to remain the real repository of governmental authority in the country. Even the ministers find themselves ineffective in the face of the monolithic force of the civil service. Their dependence on the latter is nearly total, and the civil servants are aware of the politicians' ultimate dependence. Lacking knowledge of details of administration, its processes and minutiae, the ministers and other politicians can ill-afford to estrange and alienate civil servants. It is, even today, the civil service that is seen to rule India albeit under the outer garb of democracy, and the most powerful element in the civil service is the class of 'baboos' (clerks) who wield the real authority at the micro-level.

A very large share of the problems and issues brought to the national legislator falls within the field of the state governments for his constituency needs, and indeed his political longevity seems to rest, to no small extent, on his capacity to remain on good terms with the political leadership of the state, particularly with the chief ministers. The chief ministers also realize this position of the MPs;

indeed they make use of the MPs to further their personal prospects and also the interests of the state government at the central level in its bid for larger shares of the central bounties. The chief ministers are known to convene meetings of the MPs coming from their states and thus organise MP lobbies at the national level. Some states in India command powerful MP lobbies in the centre, and no discussion of federalism in India can be considered to be complete without an analysis of the role that they have come to play in the field of centre-state relations.

4

THE MINISTER AND THE CIVIL SERVANT

PARLIAMENTARY DEMOCRACY brings into operation a particular political arrangement which entrusts the country's administrative system including its resources, both human and material, to the people's elected representatives who, thus mandated, carry on the tasks of governance for the period for which they are elected. This group of people, the political executive, is under an obligation to ensure the continued performance of current functions and enforcement of existing laws and rules, and, in addition, the accomplishment of goals and objectives it had itself outlined before the electorate. No political executive in the twentieth century inherits a completely clean slate to start on, and soon after taking the oath of office it discovers that inherited a large body of laws, rules, progrommes, functions, and responsibilities, which it is under an obligation to enforce and execute (unless annulled) and to which it is also called upon to add. Even the most radically inclined political party coming to power in the Union Government inherits over 1,500 Central statutes, a large number of them had been enacted by the British, and it builds on them by taking up new tasks and initiating new measures it has promised to the electorate.

In addition, the political executive gets the legacy of the administrative system which indeed becomes automatically the instrument for the implementation of its programmes and policies. The term 'administrative system' refers to all those institutions and offices created under the governmental and quasi-governmental control as well as the personnel manning and operating them. It is a huge and expanding machine employing a large manpower possessing varied skills and competence. The administrative system at the Central level alone employs, for instance, over three million persons and they constitute the permanent executive—permanent because while the members of the political executive are temporary, coming into public office and going out of it depending upon the electoral verdict, they are recruited on the basis of a set of objective criteria and, besides are expected to serve and service the political executive with utmost devotion, competence and impartiality. It is this faith which sustains and brightens up parliamentarianism. One cannot do better than quote Earl Attlee, the Prime Minister of Britain, who succeeded Winston Churchill but inherited the civil service which had worked under his political opponent, many members of which were even appointed by him.

> When I succeeded Mr. Churchill as Prime Minister and returned to the conference at Potsdam, I took with me precisely the same team of civil servants, including even the principal secretary, as had served my predecessor. This occasioned a lively surprise among our American friends who were accustomed to the American system whereby the leading official advisers of the President and of the members of his Cabinet are usually of his and their own colour. This incident brought out forcibly the very special position of the British Civil Service, a position which has developed during the past hundred years as the result of the Trevelyan-Northcote reforms.[1]

He continued :

> I do not think that this remarkable attribute of impartiality in the British Civil Service is sufficiently widely known nor adequately recognised for what is—one of the strongest bulwarks of democracy. I am often at pains to point this out and did so at a recent conference of Asiatic socialists in Rangoon where I told them, to their surprise, that the same men who had worked out the details of Labour's Transport Act were now, at the behest of a Conservative Government, engaged in pulling it to pieces.[2]

Political Executive

Democracy postulates a kind of hierarchical arrangement placing the political executive at the top of the administrative system which is obliged to function as an instrument of the former to carry out its policies and programmes—no less than to enforce the existing laws, implement the on-going programmes and carry out myriad functions.

1. C.R. Attlee, "Civil Servants, Ministers, Parliament and these Public", *Indian Journal of Public Administration*, Vol. 1, No. 2, April-June 1955, p. 95.
2. Ibid, p. 95.

The relationship between the political executive and the permanent executive necessarily depends upon the form of democracy the society has opted for. The parliamentary democracy postulates a particular kind of relationship, which is unlike that obtaining under the presidential system of government. In India the political executive is the council of ministers with the prime minister at its head, but in reality it is the cabinet, a smaller body consisting of the more senior members of the council of ministers. The cabinet, functioning on the principle of collective responsibility, is the top policy-making body in the government and exercises control over the entire machinery of government and public personnel. To transact its business it ordinarely meets once a week and more often depending upon circumstances. The political executive's control over administration is continuous and all pervasive. The cabinet, as already mentioned, is the top policy-making body and it controls the permanent executive by virtue of this position and the functions which flow from it. It has, subject to the compliance with constitutional formalities, the power of appointment and removal of personnel and of issuing directions to ensure proper execution. It particularly exercises surveillance and control over the machinery of government by obliging the following matters to come before it for decision :

(i) Cases involving legislation including the issue of ordinances.
(ii) Addresses and messages of the President to Houses of Parliament.
(iii) Cases involving negotiations with foreign and commonwealth countries on treaties, agreements and other important matters.
(iv) Cases relating to proclamation of emergency under Articles 352-360 of the Constitution and other matters related thereto.
(v) Cases relating to commencement or cessation of a state of war and related matters.
(vi) Proposals relating to : (a) creation of new corporations or companies wholly owned by Central Government or a public sector undertaking in providing share capital to a new or any existing corporation or company ; (c) winding up, amalgamation, or such other major schemes of structural reorganisation of public sector undertakings.
(vii) Cases in which a difference of opinion arises between two or more ministers and a cabinet decision is desired.

(viii) Cases in which a committee of cabinet or its chairman desires a decision or direction of cabinet in a matter of importance on a subject assigned to its charge.

(ix) Cases having financial implications on which the finance minister desires a decision of the cabinet.

(x) Proposals to vary or reverse a decision previously taken by the cabinet.

(xi) Any other case which the President or the Prime Minister may by a general or special order require to be brought before the cabinet.

Matters other than these fall within the spheres of individual ministers. Here also not all kinds of business need come to the minister for his direct handling and disposal. Indeed, there are well-defined internal rules regarding the levels of decision-making, leaving only the more important items of work to be decided by the minister. These rules, however, do not restrict his powers and position, and he is at liberty to decide himself on any item of work falling under his political charge. He, moreover, enjoys the right to issue directives and instructions to the public personnel under his charge.

The minister's responsibilities are numerous and varied and of a delicate nature and in order to make a dent on the system he must learn to view his role in a perspective. He is to lay down policies on subjects falling under his charge, ensure their effective implementation and, besides, provide drive and leadership to those working under him. He has under his command an administrative structure and he must delegate functions to his administrative subordinates. He should as a rule make only general decisions and avoid interesting himself in particular decisions, which instead should be left to the administrative hierarchies for handling.

Such, then, are the general responsibilities of the ministers in a parliamentary system of government and though these have gradually crystallised first in Britain, they constitute the essential ingredients of the parliamentary system of government as obtain in India—indeed wherever it prevails. In India, however, ministers have not shown any marked inclination to restrict themselves to such general policy-meking roles and instead have been increasingly interesting themselves in particular cases. This practice, first emanating at the State level but since seventies taken recourse to even at the Central level, has become fairly widespread entailing grave dysfunctionalities for the political system.

PERMANENT EXECUTIVE

The functions of the permanent executive, the civil service, are broadly twofold. One is the 'staff' function which, for instance, is performed in the secretariat where the civil servants' responsibilities consist in assisting the minister in policy-making. It is appropriate to quote Sir Warren Fisher who defined, with enviable brevity and lucidity, the minister-civil service relationship while tendering evidence before the Tomlin Commission on the Civil Service in Britain (1929-31) :

> Determination of policy is the function of minister and once a policy is determined it is the unquestioned and unquestionable business of the civil servant to strive to carry out that policy with precisely the same energy and precisely the same goodwill whether he agrees with it. . . . That is axiomatic and will never be in dispute. At the same time it is the traditional duty of civil servants, while decisions are being formulated, to make available to their political chief all the information and experience at their disposal, and to do this without fear or favour, irrespective of whether the advice thus tendered may accord or not with the minister's initial view. The presentation to the minister of relevant facts, the ascertainment and marshalling of which may often call into play the whole organisation of a department, demands of the civil servant the greatest care. The presentation of inferences from the facts equally demands from him all the wisdom and all the detachment he can command.
> The preservation of integrity, fearlessness, and independence of thought ând utterance in their private communion with ministers of the experienced officials selected to fill the top posts in the service is an essential principle in enlightened government ; as whether or not ministers accept the advice his advice frankly placed at their disposal, and acceptance or rejection of such advice is extensively a matter for their judgement—it enables them to be assured that their decisions are reached only after the relevant facts and the various considerations have, so far as the machinery of government can secure, been definitely brought before their minds[3].

It may be pointed out that a political party when it comes into power has with it only general ideas of the policies it wishes to

3. *Royal Commission on the Civil Service : Minutes of Evidence*, London H.M.S.O., 1931, p. 1268.

follow. It has not till then worked out the details of the policies nor the mechanisms of the manner in which to execute them. This is the case even with the political parties in the West. In India, the policy announcements of the political parties are even feebler and vaguer giving hardly any meaningful clue to what they would exactly do and in what manner. This happens because, among others, they do not have effective policy planning cells or research wings to engage in policy-making, as is the case with the political parties in the West. More often than not, personal predelictions, even idiosyncrasies of individual political leaders pass for what get known as policies. The expert knowledge required for transforming such policies into actionable programmes, backed by the necessary laws, rules, regulations and directives is as a rule made available by the civil servants working in the secretariat. It is their professional duty to tender the advice to the minister without fear and based on the highest standards of competence and integrity. They must point out to the minister the implications and the consequences of the policy he proposes to adopt. However, once the policy is decided by him they must from then onwards address themselves to the task of its efficient execution.

It is worth mentioning here that both the political executive and the permanent executive are subject to the constitution and the laws of the land, and no one, however, exalted be his office, can act illegally and immorally. What this means in this specific context is that the civil servants located in the secretariat are the minister's advisers and aides, but they must conduct themselves within the four corners of the laws of the land.

The staff functions have a strong resemblance with the legislative task. It is as we know the recognised function of a legislature to enact laws while it is the task of the secretariat personnel to frame rules and regulations to make them actionable. There does not thus exist any essential difference between the writing of a law and the writing of rules and regulations.

Besides, the civil service has the 'line' function also, which is performed by what are called the attached and subordinate offices in the Union Government and directorates and district administration in the States. As briefly referred to at the start of the present chapter, the civil service implements the laws and executes the various plans and programmes. This sphere of civil service action, it must be noted, lies outside the direct manipulation by the minister, for the public functionaries operating in this area derive their authority from specific laws figuring on the statute book, and they are personally accountable for the manner of execution.

The line function which the civil servants are called upon to perform acquires the colour of a quasi-judicial work. The field level public personnel in a way apply the laws to particular cases and here the source of authority is the law, not the minister. A superintendent of police, for instance, has to decide whether to prosecute a person on the basis of facts available to him and while engaged in such an analysis he is applying a law to the facts before him in the same way as a judge.

This line of analysis is important and must register itself with both the ministers and the civil servant. The minister's authority is ordinarily supreme (subject to the constitution and norms of public morality) in the staff functions, but not so in the area of administrative action where line functions are performed. These two fields of activities must not be confused or mixed.

OPERATIONAL REALITY

The minister, it has been noted is the policy-making authority, and the civil servants posted in the secretariat are to advise him in this respect. In practice, however, there is a reluctance on his part to welcome correct advice and, what is more, the civil servants too on their part are turning sycophants and giving the kind of counsel which would please the minister showing not much concern for public interest. One may, for instance, note the following comment made by the Administrative Reforms Commission (1966-72) though there is a steep deterioration in this relationship since then :

> There is a disinclination among quite a number of ministers to welcome frank and impartial advice from the secretary or his aides and an inclination to judge him by his willingness to do what they wish him to do. Instances are not wanting of ministers preferring a convenient subordinate to a strong one and thereby making the latter not only ineffective but a sulky and unwilling worker. This has also bred a tendency on the part of an increasing number of civil servants to attempt to anticipate the minister's wishes and proffer their advice accordingly. A further development of this unhealthy trend is the emergence of personal affiliations leading to an element of 'politicalisation' among the civil servants. All these cut at the root of the healthy

relationship. The Prime Minister should take special interest to curb this tendency, with the assistance of the cabinet secretary and the central personnel agency.[4]

The minister, generally speaking, does not work at his proper level and interests himself in line functions as well as personnel matters. Almost all ministers, today, betray an obsession with matters like individual postings, transfers, promotions and similar acts of patronage ; and management of civil service postings and transfers appears to be the only 'creative' activity in several governments and several departments in India. This aspect of ministerial behaviour has attracted adverse comments from the successive administrative reform committees, but instead of this habit disappearing or remaining under control, it has become even more deeply entrenched in the in the contemporary political life in the country. It is instructive to read the following letter written by a minister in Punjab to the legislators of his State.

> While I am anxious to exchange views with my colleague legislators on day-to-day problems and equally anxious to ensure, as far as possible, that their constituencies are properly looked after, at least in so far as the departments which fall in my portfolio are concerned, I have felt that most of my time in office is being spent on conversations and in listening to grievances and complaints of the individuals who accompany legislators or come alone. The practice of running to a minister on minor matters, which could be attended to and which have ultimately to be referred to local officers for disposal, seems lately to have grown out of all proportions, with the result that :
>
> 1. Most of the local officers do not properly attend to complainants who go to them independently. As the number of references to these officers from ministers on routine matters have greatly increased, they have lost their due importance which perhaps once they had :
> 2. Most of the time of the ministers is spent on attending to each individual and little or no time in office or at their residence is left for files which go on accumulating and do not receive proper attention. Very little time is left for original thinking, for chalking out schemes for improving working of the departments under their charge.

4. *Report on the Machinery of the Government of India and its Procedures of Work*, New Delhi, Administrative Reforms Commission, 1968, para 56.

> You will appreciate that if I do not devote sufficient time to dispose of files or think of new schemes aimed at the general uplift of the masses, I shall be failing in my duty as minister to the country, to the State and to you also who have put me on this chair. True, I may succeed in shifting a petty official from one place to another or even secure justice to an individual, but in the large context I shall have not done my duty. This feeling has been pricking my conscience and this feeling has compelled me to write this letter to you in the hope that you will cooperate with me in this matter. We must educate the before it masses, is too late, to get things done in a regulated manner. The people should approach the legislators only when they have exhausted all the sources prescribed in the law or under rules. The legislators, in turn, should approach the ministers after they have failed to get a problem settled in consultation with the local officers concerned and they feel that the importance of the issue to the general public is such as warrants a discussion with the minister. I would request you to write to me and apprise me of the problem, after which I shall be too glad to fix up a time with you, so that we should be able to have a thorough discussion with the help of material with Government and arrive at a decision which may not have to be changed the next morning, as it is happening in many cases. I again assure you of my utmost consideration to you and assistance in all matters but only expect you to cooperate with me so far as method of approach is concerned. I have said all this in the general interest of the State.[5]

While, therefore, public administration feels the presence of the politician-minister at the wrong place it does not get from him what he is expected to provide, namely, public policies. Only a very small number of the several hundred ministers presently holding office at the Centre and in the States appear to concern themselves with policy-making. Most of them have made it a habit to perform line functions and thus decide particular cases. Especially in the State, a very large number of ministers have little aptitude for policy making but evince unbounded interest in particular cases.

The reasons for the ministers not observing the correct course of action which is considered to be normal in the maturer democracies appear to be the following :

5. *Report of the Punjab Administrative Reforms Commission*, Chandigarh, Controller of Printing & Stationery, Government of Punjab, 1966, pp 64-5.

1. It requires knowledge, intelligence and perseverance to make public policies. Most ministers lack the ability to comprehend policy implications, much less articulate them.
2. In contrast, it is much easier to decide particular cases, more so when such decisions are to be ad hoc in nature.
3. The kind of minister holding political power today is generally innocent of the rule of law, the bedrock of democracy. A product of adult franchise in a predominnantly illiterate environment, he is deeply imbued with the native political culture according to which the ruler is all powerful, his will is law, and there is no check on his powers.
4. The elected representatives in India carry exaggerated notions about themselves and their position in the poiltical system. It is common for the legislators to claim all kinds of privileges and for the ministers to insist upon absolute authority over matters constitutionally under his charge. This is contrary to the theory and practice of parliamentary democracy as operating in maturer societies. But such a notion has gained widespread currency in the country and the minister does not fully recognise the limitedness of his brief.
5. It is by deciding the individual cases that the minister builds up both a support structure and a resource structure for himself. He is able to oblige persons, build up contacts, and meet caste, communal and regional pressures. Political corruption has been thriving in India precisely because of ministers' indulgence in individual cases for granting of favour—or frown. The linkage politics, characteristic of present day Indian politics, owes itself primarily to the propensity on the part of the ministers to decide particular cases.

Such wrong priorities of the minister have produced imbalances and dysfunctionalities in the country's political system. The professional norms of the bureaucracy have suffered serious erosion, and a general climate of normlessness prevails all round. The minister has been able to accomplish all this because of the triple powers at his disposal : (i) power of transfer, (ii) power of suspension, and (iii) power to give accelerated promotion or deny promotion.

It is clear that when one joins the civil service one has to take in one's stride the post that may be offered. It is exactly this which many civil servants are not mentally prepared to accept, and it is precisely here that the ministers make interventions. The civil servants are inordinately choosy in this regard and, what is more, the resourceful among them even succeed in getting plum posts in Delhi and other metropolitan places. It is this knowledge of the civil servants' weakness that the minister uses to serve his political and personal ends. He obliges them by giving them postings of their likings, and, as its quid pro quo, the latter too learn to reciprocate.

Many reasons account for the bureaucratic reluctance to take transfers stoically. First, the contemporary administrative culture of India tends to make too much of a distinction between various posts and so a recently recruited civil servant undergoes a particular socialisation process and begins to manipulate postings and transfers right from the start of his career. Secondly, there are several 'wet' posts in administration which are very attractive to civil servants and which also carry a premium. Such posts are filled up through the politics of manipulation. Thirdly, there is, rightly or wrongly, a widespread feeling among the civil servants that, in order to survive and swim one needs to have a godfather in politics and they make a special effort to cultivate the influential (which means unscrupulous) politicians for their own career improvement. Finally, India is not a homogeneous society with an even distribution of infrastructural facilities. Indeed, the social infrastucture is so heavily concentrated in Delhi and a few other metropolitan places that many civil servants would loath moving away from such places. Moreover, the educational system in operation in different States of India is not similar and a boy receiving his schooling in the Hindi belt would find it extremely difficult to adjust himself in a school in a different linguistic zone. As a civil servant of today generally comes from a middle class background with a limited bargaining capacity (because of acute unemployment in the country) a mere threat of a long-distance transfer tends to make him particularly vulnerable to pressures. Besides, there are many civil servants who are highly conscientious, applying the laws in an even-handed way. It is natural that they would harm certain vested interests which, thus provoked, then mobilise their resources to get them transferred-and posted at far off places. This has a demoralising effect on the bureaucracy. In short, administrative transfers and postings are no longer the functions of the chief personnel agency in the government; they have become devices available to the influential politicians to manipulate the civil servants.

A second power available to a minister to break in a civil servant is that of putting him under suspension on one pretext or the other. The Supreme Court of India has held that suspension is no punishment, and thus buttressed the minister can suspend a civil servant without having to assign any reason whatever and for as long as he wants. A civil servant, put under suspension, is apt to get completely demoralised, much more so if he is a person of integrity and character. There have been cases of senior and honest civil servants remaining under suspension for years, their fault apparently being their unwillingness to oblige the minister and to his line.

The third device at the disposal of the minister is that of awarding or denying promotions. As promotion is not considered as a right, civil servants naturally look to their superiors, including the political leadership, for such advancements. Besides, there are many plum posts in public administration which are virtually reserved for the favourite civil servants.

It is by a dexterous use of these three devices that the contemporary political leadership in India has been able to secure in practice an accommodating bureaucracy. Honest and professionaly oriented civil servants have been gradually eased out from the sanctum sanctorum of administration and posted in the administrative periphery while the pliable and the pliant ones find themselves planted at all strategic positions.

The above is perhaps too one-sided an account of the civil service made to wilt under the political pressures. How does the political leadership gain by administrative transfers if the bureaucracy is truly professional ? A civil servant's successor would in that case equally uphold the laws and the rules and show no signs of succumbing to political blandishments. The minister would then realise before long the futility of the game of shifting public functioharies to and fro. The distressing fact today is that the civil service has lost its elan and is itself not professional, ready to do anything or everything—in the expectation of a reward, or for fear of, say, transfers. The various commissions of inquiry set up by both the central and state governments have dutifully confirmed the existence of civil servants who have little bothered about the prevalent laws and professional poperiety and freely aligned themselves with the political executive in cynical disregard of public interest. They pander to the wishes of their superiors in a desire to secure protection for themselves. Highly selective in their response patterns, they feel no compunction in bending backwards to do what is required by those in a position to oblige or 'punish' them. Rules may get interpreted favourably, precedents are overlooked and administrative wheels begin to move with fantastic speed. But the same administrator operates at a snail's pace when a common man goes to him for even the most legitimate work. It would be utterly naive to cast the civil servants in the image of reluctant sinners ; they are willing, on occasions, even leading, partners in the shady deals. The ministers and the civil servants respond to each other's agenda.

CONCLUDING OBSERVATIONS

The bureaucracy in India is thus bearing the brunt of two kinds of politics—politics from without and from within. All strategic positions in public administration are increasingly getting reserved only for those who have their spokesmen among the influential politicians or senior bureaucrats, for, where the politician leaves, they take over. The civil service in India is not homogeneous ; it has factions based on regionalism, casteism, or service memberships, all obsessed with manipulation of postings and promotions and matters of personal advancement. All taken together, a civil servant who is devoted only to his work, and performs it impartially, discovers himself to be completely isolated and before long finds himself consigned to the administrative periphery with little hope of retrieval.

The relationship between the ministers and the civil servants has come to be characterised by a growing feeling of uneasiness, even suspicion and a civil servant's uppermost consideration, today, is to play safe and to show only routine initiative and drive in his work. This breeds a tendency for over-consultation and most matters are pushed upward for decision-making. In years to come, politics in India is likely to become both more intensive, aggressive and multilinear accompanied by an increasing traditionalisation of itself, largely as a result of the emergence of new political leadership thrown up by the contemporary political and electoral processes. The civil service, consequently, is apt to face new and novel pressures and in more concentrated dosages ; and in the process Max Weber would be discovered to be nearly totally irrelevant. It appears that India is on its way to evolving an Eastminster model of role relationship between the political executive and the permanent executive.

It is obviously too harsh and untrue to ascribe this kind of behaviour to the totality of the civil service. There are civil servants noble and devoted and they would be the pride of even the most advanced administration in the world. One may say that between ten to twenty per cent of the higher civil servants may be put in the category of deviants behaving in the way as reported by the various commissions of inquiry. Between one-fourth and one-third of the mandarins are totally dedicated, conscientious and morally upright. The remaining segment of the higher civil service, which is nearly half of the total number of senior public personnel, would ordinarily like to act according to established rules and regulations, distinctly standing apart from the first enumeration yet not falling in the second category of personnel. They would not collude with the ministers nor would they at the same time dare collide with them. They read the 'weather reports' rather minutely and prune their conduct suitably so that they do not get drenched. If the political leadership is itself wanting in integrity they would move closer to the first category ; if it is strict, they would be found to be nearer to the second category.

5

THE PARTY SYSTEM

POLITICAL PARTIES are the legitimate agents of interest articulation and aggregation, and have a critically important role in the functioning of a democratic political system, even though the constitution may not take cognizance of them. The Indian Constitution, for instance, does not anywhere refer to political parties much less formally recognise them and endow them with definite functions. Yet the fact is that parties are the life-lines of Indian politics. The party system in India is characterised, more than anything else, by a high degree of pluralism. Six political parties are listed by the Election Commission as national parties and as many as 27 as state ones covering a wide spectrum. One cluster includes the leftist parties consisting of the Communist Party of India, the Communist Party of India (Marxist) and other splinter groups professing various hues of the leftist ideology. At the other end of the political spectrum stand the so-called rightist parties (not a very correct label, perhaps) such as the Bhartiya Janata Party (old Jana Sangh) and, perhaps, the Lok Dal. Parties like the Congress (I), Congress (S), Congress (J), Janata Party etc. fall in the centre or towards the 'left of the centre' and may be said to form a separate cluster. The number of parties is, thus, very large, but there is one dominant party, namely the Congress Party presently under the leadership of Indira Gandhi. An equally noteworthy feature of the country's party system is its extreme fluidity. There is hardly any season of the year when talks about creation of some new party or merger of some 'like-minded' parties etc. are not heard. The only parties which have stayed stable in their membership are the communist parties and to a lesser extent the Bhartiya Janata Party because of their idological anchorage. This fluidity owes itself, atleast in part, to a craving for office in some party or the other. The political leaders in India are basically office-seekers. This should not have posed a problem if their supply were limited. Ironically, there are more leaders in India than the number of offices which could absorb them, this too resulting in the phenomenon of proliferation of parties.

A regretful feature of Indian political parties is their occasional splits and break-ups the primary motivation for which being more personal than ideological. The Congress Party was first split up in 1969, leading to the emergence of two Congresses—the Congress led by Indira Gandhi and the Congress led by the 'syndidcate'. At that time it was widely publicised as being deeply ideological but the fact is that Indira Gandhi sought to outmanoeuvre her political opponents and consolidate her power in the party. The Congress (O) was nearly completely annihilated in the election of 1971. The second split in the Congress of Indira Gandhi occurred, in January 1978, and as a result two groups emerged—one led by K. Brahmananda Reddy, the then Party President and the other by Indira Gandhi. In course of time the Indira-led Congress emerged as the real Congress Party ; and the other Congress, at no time very strong, itself suffered a split in August 1981 when Jagjivan Ram walked out of it to form his separate Congress (J).

The Janata Party, formed in 1977 as a result of the merger of the Congress (O), the Jana Sangh, the Bhartiya Lok Dal and the Socialist Party[1] could not remain united for long. It was a thinly disguised coalition of five parties, each pulling in a different direction. The Janata Party got divided in 1979, even before the completion of half the term of the Lok Sabha, necessitating the holding of fresh general election in 1980—an election in which the heroes of 1977 were made to eat the dust.

The Communist Party of India, first founded in 1928, did not escape splitting, the cause of contention being the Chinese attack on India in 1962. One section of the Communists was talking in favour of 'defence of the motherland' where as the other one was inclined to adopt a pro-Chinese attitude. In 1964 the latter group suffered suspension from the Party and the suspended group organised itself as the Communist Party of India (Marxist). In 1969 a third Communist Party—the Communist Party of India (Marxist-Leninist)—was formed by the extremist sections within the communists, its leader being Charu Majumdar of the Naxalbari fame. Indeed, there are in existence today nearly ten Naxalite groups professing differing intensities of the militant leftist ideology.

It is not correct that only national parties show susceptibility to splits and divisions. A state level party like the Dravida Munnetra

1. The Congress for Democracy merged with the the Janata Party sometime later.

Kazhagam, itself a splinter from the Dravida Kazhagam breaking away in 1949, was divided in 1972 resulting in the emergence of another party of the name of All India Anna DMK (AIADMK) under the leadership of M.G. Ramachandran, a former film actor of Tamil screen. This party is the ruling one in Tamil Nadu since 1977.

The Congress Party

The Congress Party must receive special notice for it is this party which has been steering the ship of the state since 1947 with a brief interruption. The Congress Party apparently frustrates any classificatory attempts of political scientists to fit into any one of the conventional categories. Since its inception in 1885, the Congress has been both a nationalist movement and a forum of competing interests. It has always been the ruling party at the Centre since 1947 except for 1977-80 when it sat as an opposition. In the states it has generally been the ruling party although other parties too have been holding the reins of goveranance. In 1984 the Congress is an opposition party in states like Jammu-Kashmir, Andhra Pradesh, West Bengal, Tamil Nadu, Tripura and Karnataka. The party broadly adopts 'left of the centre' policies on most problems and tries to integrate the interests of as many groups and sections of the population as possible. The party is secular but does not hesitate making compromises and striking deals with religio-communal sections for short-term gains. Its history is replete with instances of such compromises.

Till the first split in 1969, the arena of political competition in India was the Congress 'system' of one party dominance. The system, one may recapitulate, was competitive, but one party of consensus occupied the dominant position in it. The Congress Party, one must stress, was a party of consensus, ever anxious to integrate the various shades of opinion existing under its umbrella. Thc opposition parties existed in large numbers but did not operate as alternative to the Congress : they were ever destined to remain at the periphery, being but the parties of pressure.

The one party dominance system of India was characterized by two notable features. First, the Congress itself was a kind of 'coalition', a conglomeration of groups and factions which had the effect of making the party all the more representative of the country's diversities in its composition. At the same time, this feature sustained competitiveness within the Party. As no single group within the Congress could remain in the ruling position indefinitely, it fostered flexibility of attitude and even rotation of office-holders. The 'musical chair' description of the Congress Party was an apt one.

Secondly, like the states in India having their separate 'bhawans' in Delhi, each opposition party had its 'bhawan', so to speak, within the Congress Party. After all, most opposition parties had the Congress as their mother party having branched out of it at some time or the other. The Congress Socialists were the first to leave the Congress, the year being 1948. After some time Acharya Kripalani and his followers left to form the Kisan Mazdoor Praja Party (KMPP) in 1951. While the streaming out process did not stop each leaver maintained a dealing point—an ideologically congruent group—in the Congress. This in its turn had a twofold effect. The opposition parties had their dealing points within the Congress and thus they sought to pressurize and influence the Congress 'system' in its decision-making processes. Also, because of the existence of such internal dealing points the Congress could absorb political leaders and groups from outside the Party. At any rate, the Congress Party had an apparently unlimited capacity of co-option and pre-emption of the opposition.

The Congress thus learnt to live with its internal contradictions ; it had a built-in opposition within itself and battles used to be fought within the Party when decisions on important national issues were concerned. It learnt to balance several interests and several levels of consciousness. It avoided ideological sharpness for its method of decision-making was essentially consensual.

The Congress 'system' was continually responding to these internally generated pressures and as a consequence it always showed remarkable flexibility in its policies and practices. The internal contradictions of the party dutifully reflected themselves in the contradictions in its programmes, particularly at the stage of implementation.

Also, the Congress was recruiting new social and economic elements in the society. Its capacity to attract them increased enormously as a direct result of the resources and power as a ruling party it had.

The split of 1969 was the first measure to re-design the Congress, and in years to come the character of the party was fast undergoing a change. The emergence of Sanjay Gandhi in the seventies further accelerated the process of change, and as a result the party was becoming more personalised than programmatic, more leader-oriented than ideological. Sanjay Gandhi's influence in party recruitment as in many other areas was very substantial. It is common knowledge that he wielded the greatest influence in the allotment of tickets to the assembly and parliamentary condidates for elections of 1980. The percentage of 'Sanjay nominees' varied from state to state but every where it was significant. In U.P., it is said that sixty per cent of the Congress (1) tickets were given to those Sanjay had nominated. In the parliamentary elections of 1980 it has been estimated that as many as 150 Sanjay candidates were nominated even though only about 80 were able to win the election. Almost without any exception, these new recruits to politics have been persons without any previous experience of work at local levels or in other spheres. They, moreover, look upon politics as a career—to earn their livelihood from it. In India nearly eighty per cent of the MPs are full-time politicians. The Congress has undergone a complete transformation from its former self. The pilot of the Congress Party has changed ; the crew has changed and so are its contents.

The Congress of Mahatma Gandhi and Nehru could not be regarded as a party, strictly speaking, being but a conglomerate of diverse interests and disparate elements. Nor can it be legitimately considered as a party today, built as it is around just one person, albeit of extra-ordinary mobilisational capabilities, signifying extreme personalisation of strategic power and authority. One has only to go through the following resolution of the Congress Legislature Party soon after the 1980 election : 'This meeting of the Party unanimously elects Mr. Sanjay Gandhi a progressive leader with a pragmatic approach, as it sincerely feels (that) he can properly guide the State's destiny and lead it to its cherished goals. In case, however, if the Prime Minister in her capacity as the A.I.C.C. (I) president feels that, in the larger national interest, his valuable services cannot be spared for U.P., the Party requests her to nominate any other suitable person who will be deemed to have been duly elected as leader of the House enjoying the Party's wholehearted and unanimous support'.[2] This resolution is quoted here merely to vividify this powerful component of the Congress culture, namely, a total subordination to the leader at the top. No other member of the party. howsoever strong or important, feels confidence in himself to think. Such a trait inhibits party-building and is dangerous at least in the long run for the party as well as for the nation. The burdens on Indira Gandhi are unimaginably heavy, for she is the party. She is the only political leader in India having the capacity of making a

2. Quoted in S. Sahay : 'Close Look : Period of Transition', *The Statesman*, 12 June, 1980.

direct appeal to the people across the land. The popular goodwill which she enjoys—and enlists—is enormous. It is no surprise that she is looked upon as the greatest vote gatherer for the party. The electoral campaigns she undertakes would simply tire out other politicians, but she is of a different mettle. Also, she possesses the political acumen as no one else has and keeps her opponents off balance. Besides, she also chooses chief ministers and other ministers in the states once her party returns to power and must also protect them, though not absolutely, from dissidents. Personal strength is not necessarily the strength of the Congress Party. The Congress Party is heavily faction-ridden at the state level, and this flows atleast partly, from the very nature of the Party itself. Being the ruling party it is a haven for people with differing orientations, dispositions, and persuasions, and what is more, they are welcome too. The reward system in the Party is so structured that no important group is left out of power for long. The chief minister of a Congress-ruled state is seldom able to complete his full term of five years, which keeps factional ambitions alive. Also the factions keep a check over the chief minister who is thus prevented from consolidating his political position in the state. The various factions are tolerated in the party because they profess their allegiance to the top leader besides performing the function of checks and balances.

The preceding discussion acquires added significance if one recalls that historically and sociologically the traits of the party do affect the decision-making style of all parties of the land. This occurs because the Congress has acted, not on its own choice, as a reference group for other parties, atleast at the sub-conscious level. It is thus not unlikely that the practices of the Congress tend to become a kind of precedents for the party system of India.

It is most notable that the Congress Party (I) is the only all-India party today even though the Election Commission of India lists six parties as 'national parties' : The Congress Party (I), the Congress Party (S), the Communist Party India, the Communist Party of India (Marxist), the Janata Party, and the Janata Party (Secular)[3]. The Congress (I) commands majority at the centre and in states such as Assam, Bihar, Haryana, U.P., M.P., Rajasthan, Orissa, Maharashtra and Gujarat where as it is in opposition in many states including West Bengal, Tamil Nadu, Andhra Pradesh, Karnataka, etc. Moreover, the Party's bastions of power and influence appear to be getting gradually attenuated. Internal dissensions are rife in all the

3. Later merged to become the Lok Dal

states. It is not securely placed even in its traditional stronghold like Maharashtra largely because of the adverse publicity given to the acts of omission and commission of men of questionable integrity like A.R. Antulay and Ramlal Adik. Early in 1984, the Congress (I) Legislature Party in Maharashtra wanted to amend the Prevention of Corruption Act to save the former Chief Minister, A.R. Antulay, from the clutches of law. Though the amendment of the anti-graft law was not carried out in deference to mounting opposition the image of the party suffered grievously. Ramlal Adik, the deputy chief minister of Maharashtra, is alleged to have misbehaved with the air hostesses of Air India while on way to West Germany to attend an international trade fair early in 1984. How can the Congress be trusted if persons of such character succeed in moving to the top and controlling its affairs was a question agitating the people. The Party has, moreover, to fight a double battle : it has to fight with the opposition as well as some of its own partymen who do not hesitate in working for the opposition's victory.

OPPOSITION

The term 'opposition' is usually applied to refer to all non-Congress (I) parties in the country even though the fact is that even the Congress (I) was an opposition party 1977-80 ; and many parties traditionally dubbed as opposition are presently running governments in states like West Bengal, Tamil Nadu, Andhra Pradesh, Karnataka, Jammu-Kashmir etc. This means that the Congress Party (I) is the ruling Party at the Centre but an opposition party in several states. We would here go by the common (even though not very correct) usage of the term 'opposition' equating it with the non-Congress (I) parties.

The line of demarcation between the ruling party and the opposition parties is rather thin and weak. This is not only because a party may be performing the ruling role at one level and an opposing one at another level of the government but also because of striking similarity in the manner of its functioning. In India the political parties do not show any perceptible degree of responsibility while sitting in opposition and this attribute is equally applicable to the Congress (I). This party is the ruling party at the Centre and as such is expected to be much more circumspect and sober in the manner of its functioning as an opposition in states like Jammu-Kashmir, West Bengal, Karnataka, etc. But the fact is that one can hardly find a more irresponsible opposition party than the Congress (I) in these states : it is not psychologically reconciled to its opposition role and to some other party's right also to rule. In another sense also one may say that the very logic of power fosters an attitude towards pragmatism and thus viewed the ideologically-oriented parties tend to lose much of their uniqueness. The CPM is a case in point. This party is ruling West Bengal and Kerala more or less like any other 'bourgeois' democratic party would generally do. Nor is the way of functioning of the Telegu Desam Government in Andhra Pradesh qualitatively different from the way of functioning of its 'extremely corrupt' predecessor-government. Conformism is fostered by the constitution no less than by the compulsions of governance and the instrumentalities of execution.

The opposition in India is highly fragmented and weak and consequently irresponsible and ineffective despite it being generally noisy. Having bilthly splintered themselves into an unmanageably large number of parties many of them began to realise a need to come together to brighten their prospccts at the hustings. Two forces seem to have triggered off the centripetal urge in them. The Congress Party has been forming the government ever since 1952 on less than fifty per cent votes. Because there are too many opposition parties their votes get split up, which gladdens the Congress heart. Empirically also it has been proved that the opposition won when it united itself against the Congress as in 1977. The non-Communist opposition parties have been addressing themselves to this question for a long time, and the search has taken at least three paths : to seek 'functional unity', whatever this may mean operationally ; to forge alliance or a united front ; or complete merger. Early in 1982 the Janata Party, the Lok Dal and the Bhartiya Janata Party, began to talk about functional unity,[4] which was construed to be a prelude to complete merger in course of time. The beginning in this direction was made by the opposition leaders coming together and addressing joint rallies. Early in 1982 the Congress (S), Lok Dal and BJP leaders shared the same platform to address a mass meeting in Haryana. Sometime later, Jagjivan Ram of Congress (J) and Charan Singh of Lok Dal jointly addressed a public meeting. In April 1982 a two-day convention was held at Chandigarh to forge opposition unity[5], and the venue of the meeting was significantly called 'Ekta Nagar' ('Unity Town'). All these efforts failed largely because of the personalised nature of Indian politics but the unexpected and

4. *The Tribune*, 9 January, 1982.
5. *The Statesman*, 17 April 1982.

thumping victory of the regional Telegu Desam Party in Andhra Predesh early in 1983 intensified unity moves among the opposition, the initiative in this regard coming from the new entrants to politics. N.T. Rama Rao, the film actor-turned chief minister of Andhra Pradesh, convened an all-party meeting at Vijayawada in May 1983 attended by as many as 24 leaders from 14 opposition parties.[6] Addressing the conclave, N.T. Rama Rao emphasized, in his own characteristic way, the need for a new 'political brotherhood' to fight the threat to national unity arising from 'the failure of the ruling party at the Centre to find timely and acceptable solution' to the urgent problems of the country and its different areas. On the question of the merger of parties, N.T. Rama Rao most significantly said :

> This is the unanimous voice of all the parties that let us not stress now on an alternative to the Congress-I. We have to first understand each other.

The Vijayawada conclave received wide publicity, and its real contribution lay in the fact that opposition parties learnt to meet together when need arose even if only to trade in platitudes. They met again in June 1983 at Delhi to keep the unity dialogue going though nothing tangible flowed from it. The conclave politics was appearing wearisome, and BJP and the Lok Dal sprang a surprise on the entire opposition as well as the ruling Congress-I by forming the National Democratic Alliance (NDA) in August 1983. The conclave politics was not proving to be much productive of definite results and parties were giving up the idea of 'a national alternative' to the ruling Congress Party despite their fondness for it. Alliance politics' was thus on their cards. An 'alliance', has rather modest pretensions : in practice, it is not much better than electoral arrangements to avoid splitting up of opposition votes. Under the terms of their agreement, the Lok Dal and the BJP remain separate organisations outside Parliament though they decided to coordinate their activities on the items of a specified common programme. The coordination is also to cover election contests though the two parties retain their respective symbols. The other non-Communist opposition parties did not wish to remain behind ; and renewed efforts were mounted to form an

6. *The Times of India*, 29 May 1983. The major parties were : J & K National Conference, Akali Dal, Rashtriya Sanjay Manch, BJP, Janata Party, Democratic Socialist Party, CPM, CPI, Congress (J), Rashtriya Congress, AIADMK and Telegu Desam.

alliance among themselves. In September 1983 the Janata Party, the Congress (S), the Democratic Socialist Party and the Rashtriya Congress, joined hands with each other and announced the formation of the United Democratic Front.

The party system of the country, thus, consists of the ruling Congress (I) Party, the National Democratic Alliance of Lok Dal—BJP and the United Front of Janata, Congress (S), Democratic Socialist Party and the Rashtriya Congress. The NDA is a combine of the Gangetic plain—or of the Hindi-belt, to put it directly. The United Front built around Janata, however has a wider base and its appeal extends to areas outside the Hindi belt also. But the Lok Dal and the BJP are structurally more cohesive and solid.

While the alliance-making was on, the conclave politics too, did not abate. The third meeting of the opposition parties was held at Srinagar in the first week to October 1983. The organisers did not originally invite the NDA which felt offended and which then decided to boycott it even though it was later invited and a personal request to attend was made. The leaders of the opposition parties discussed the centre-state relations but could not explore the possibility of formation of a broad-based non-Congress (I) front. The boycott of thc conclave by the NDA deprived it of much its meaning, for it effectively foiled the prospect of unity among the non-Congress (I) parties or of the emergence of a credible alternative to the ruling party. But the idea of the conclave was not debunked. The fourth meeting took place in Calcutta early in January 1984, and the attendance was still further attenuated. The process of discrimination which had surfaced at Srinagar was reinforced and institutionalised at Calcutta, in the sense that the AIADMK of M.G. Ramachandran was added to the list of non-invitees. The NDA was also kept out. This set at naught the basic purpose of conclave politics.

Indian political system has always been characterised by a multiplicity of parties. It was only during 1977-79 that their number dwindled, and it seemed at the time that India was on way to developing a kind of two party system. During 1977-81 a burgeoning of political parties was witnessed, and again, India was back to a 'square one', so to speak. This is notwithstanding the fact that efforts are made from time to time to evolve a united opposition or a federation of parties, the motivation being a sheer desire to dislodge the Congress (I) from the seat of power. The previous experience has convinced them that when they got united and fought the ruling Congress Party jointly they have carried the day. There is thus a force driving them towards unity, but the effort singularly lacks emotional jacking up. The feelings of pride and prejudice are deeply ingrained in them, which keeps them apart notwithstanding their occasional forays into opposition summitry.

Ironically, the opposition parties, even when united, begin to distance themselves from each other once the election has been won : the process of disintegration closely follows the success at the hustings. This is because the constituent units begin to press for the lion's share of loaves and fishes of office for their erstwhile groups. Indeed, the unity moves themselves are not very honest, for the opposition leaders begin to seek 'key posts' even before the 'unity' decisions are taken.

The organisational structures of political parties in India are weak, and nowhere is this weakness more marked than at the grossroots level. Party polls are not regularly held, inner-party democracy is not encouraged nor does it exist in any conspicuous way. All political parties including even the Communists and the Socialists are mindful of the caste and religious compositions in every constituency while fielding their candidates and this 'casteist calculus' was developed as early as 1952 when the first general election took place. Most parties are built around personalities and slogans.

A problem with parties in India is that they do not show their willingness to function within a commonly accepted framework. There are hardly any commonly accepted rules of the game and each party, consequently, looks at issues and problems from the standpoint of its own narrow, immediate personalised gains. This irresponsibility is no less characterising even the Congress (I) Party which, being the ruling party, is expected to be much more reasonable in its style and stance when sitting as an opposition. The behaviour which it wants the opposition to eschew in the Lok Sabha is exactly what itself exhibits without the slightest guilty conscience in states like Jammu-Kashmir, West Bengal, Andhra Pradesh and Karnataka. The Congress Party thinks, it is its birthright to rule, and it is just not prepared to sit as an opposition and be content to play that role honourably. It has to undergo quite a bit of unlearning if the prospects for democracy are to be made brighter. This is what is required of the opposition parties also—their sole aim, today, is to discomfit the government on each and every issue even where grave national issues are involved. The stand taken by the Janata Party and the Bhartiya Janata Party on the Punjab problem (1982-84) has been appallingly shocking, guided by no principles of national interest. One opposition leader, Subramaniam Swamy, behaved in a comic way by spending a few days in the Golden Temple at Amritsar and giving a clean certificate to the extremists. The opposition parties are under an obligation to offer principled opposition to the Government, not opportunistic opposition.

Regional parties

All India parties are in a state of decline of late and the regional parties appear to be gaining ascendancy. Even though its influence is uneven, the Congress (I) Party is the only party which is more of an all-India character than any other. The Congress (I) is not strong in Jammu-Kashmir, Punjab, Kerala, West Bengal and Tamil Nadu for a long period. The Janata Party which emerged in 1977 as a national alternative in the wake of the National Emergency, could be represented only from eight out of 22 states in India in 1980, these states being Bihar, Gujarat, Haryana, Karnataka, M.P., Maharashtra, Rajasthan, U.P. and Delhi. What this confirms is that the Janata Party is fast losing its all-India representative character.

The apparent decline of the all-India parties carries many implications for the political system of the land. The Congress Party. with all its weaknesses, remains as the only all-India party ; and with the prospect of an alternative gone it may tend to grow more arbitrary in its actions and unresponsive to public opinion on many matters. It should also be remembered that all-India parties keep an all-India vision before them while formulating their views and opinions and thus emerge as a powerful instrument of nation-building and development. The emergence of regional or state parties would indicate an ascendancy of narrow castiest and parochial forces and would thus turn back the clock of history. These parties may then weaken the national mobilisational efforts.

Yet the fact is that the enormous plurality of India makes the emergence of regional parties incscapable. What is argued here is that the number of parties need not be numerous. Regional parties seem to emerge fast, and the wind seems to be blowing in favour of 'Back to the States'. The CPM has been doing well by concentrating on West Bengal, Kerala and Tripura. Classified as a national party, it may be more realistic to view it as a regional party with strong base in these three states. The DMK and AIADMK restrict their activities to Tamil Nadu (and Pond cherry). The Akali Dal confines itself to Punjab. The Telegu Desam Party, founded on 29 March 1982 is a state party restricted to the Andhra Pradesh. The regional parties in the North-Eastern India are now a factor to be reckoned with.

The regional parties may be in a better position to articulate the individual state's grievances and view points. It is good to remember that the centralising provisions and arrangements of the Indian constitution do design a certain role for the regional parties : the latter are needed by the states to take up their issues bequeathed by the constitution. Thus viewed, it would not be far-fetched to speculate that the regional parties may become like the standing Constituent Assembly of India to demand changes in the federal provisions of the constitution and to re-write this chapter. When parties seek to be national they have to dilute their state appeal. A feeling is also growing in some far off states that the high avenues of offices are ever barred for them, for it has become the prerogrative of large-sized states like UP and Bihar to hold key offices in the Central Government. The Prime Minister of India has always come from UP (except when Morarji Desai was the Prime Minister during 1977-79). This feeling too, acts as a spurt to regionalism in India.

The regional parties may also boast of a competent leadership, far superior to what is ordinarily to be discovered in the Congress-ruled states. Few among the Congress Chief Ministers would be able to match Jyoti Basu, for instance.

The regional phenomenon may put centre-state relations under a new level of stress and it is necessary that the states are given a larger measure of automony and financial resources necessary for respectable self-management. What is more, the process of decentralisation should not stop at the state level only but be carried at the lower levels too. It is extremely desirable that the local government is also provided with a constitutional base and the constitution should be so amended as to provide a fourth list of local taxes for the excluse use of the local governments.

6

COALITION GOVERNMENT

To an average Indian, the term 'coalition government' irresistably evokes an image of instability, ineffectiveness, slowness, indecisiveness and attributes of such a negative colour. This is partly a result of British thinking on 'coalitionalism' but partly also of our own absolutely uncritical estimation of this political mechanism. To us, a two party system, with one forming the government and the other waiting in the wings, is an over-riding political virtue and a coalition is a departure from the neatness and summary of the system.

The Oxford Dictionary defines 'coalition' as a 'temporary combination for special ends between parties that retain distinctive principles'. A coalition government is a combination of two or more different political parties in order to achieve some goal which is mutually shared. The goal generally is to secure a working majority to enable the members of the coalition to form the government. But in times of crises a coalition may be formed to reduce partisan politics. There may be some other reasons also for forming a coalition.

One may also go into the question of whether a coalition government should be considered to be a necessary evil to be pressed into service only in the event of no single party commanding a legislative majority or even a desirability in itself. A coalition government is generally formed only when no one party is able to secure a majority of seats in the legislature. If a party gets a majority in the legislature it would constitute the government on its own, thus taking the full responsibility of implementing its election promises and being accountable to the people for it. It keeps in tact the clear-cut division of responsibility in a parliamentary democracy—one party forming the government the others remaining in opposition. In short, a coalition government, it is argued, is a device for special occasions—when no party is in majority or when there is national emergency calling for united efforts. It is, thus, a sub-ideal. Some political analysts seem, however, to commend coalitionalism even for normal times, their argument being that this government would be more broad-based thus reducing discord and disharmony in the society. L.P. Singh the former Governor of Assam, for instance says :

> It is arguable that coalition governments at the centre, involving sharing of governmental responsibility, might have led to greater harmonisation of diverse interests and prevented some of the acute conflicts that have arisen in certain parts of the country from time to time, or the present distrust and misunderstanding between some of the states and the centre[1].

Coalition government in the West

The Indian perception of coalition is unconsciously shaped by the British attitude and political values. Indians recall with jubilation that observation made by Disraeli, namely 'England does not love coalitions.' Harold Wilson has also commenced :

> Peace time coalitions invariably produce fudged decisions where words mean more than actions, and the achievement of the lowest common denominator is regarded the highest act of coalition statemanship. Moreover, an inter-party coalition produces—is sometimes designed to produce—a paralysis of opposition. And when an important and self-conscious section of the country is denied effective parliamentary representation, frustration leads to extra-parliamentary action[2].

But one must note that Britain was coalitional more than once. The country had coalition governments during the second half of the nineteenth century as well as during 1915-1945. Winston Churchill's Government during the Second World War was a national government comprising all the main political parties. The British practice is thus not indiscriminately against alliance or partnership in government making even though the country has an established two party system.

Coalition government is much more widespread in West European countries. France, Belgium, West Germany, Holland, Denmark, Italy etc. have multiparty systems and a coalitional government is the norm rather than exception in them. Switzerland, of course, is the most outstanding example of coalition government : since 1959 it has had coalition governments uninterruptedly. All these governments

1. L.P. Singh : '*Learning from Experience*', Seminar, 298, June 1984, p. 18.
2. Quoted by L.P. Singh, *op. cit.*

have been second to none in providing political stability to the people no less than economic prosperity.

One must note that the Western countries cited about are small in size and population with cultural and social homogeneity, and, with the exception of Switzerland, are under the unitary form of government. When these countries can go coalitional the prospect of India with respect of one party commanding legislative majority to form the government becomes much less bright in view of the vastness and diversity of the country.

History of coalition governments

Coalition government acquires a relevance only in a parliamentary democracy. It is, therefore, understandable that this question could arise only when India was firmly put on the path of parliamentarism. Though a sort of parliamentary democracy in India began with the Government of India Act, 1919 the style of governance—called dyarchy—did not leave any room for coalitional inter-play. It was under the Government of India Act, 1935 that the concept of parliamentary democracy as it is understood took root and was put into operation at the provincial level. It is politically significant that in the election held in 1937 no single party could win a majority in Punjab and Sindh and both these provinces were ruled by coalitions.

There was another incident of historic significance occurring at this time. In the United Provinces, the Congress Party had acquired an absolute majority in the election held in 1937, but Mohammed Ali Jinnah expected a coalition consisting of the Congress and the Muslim League to be formed. The Congress leaders, apparently influenced by the British thinking, took the view that a coalition was thought of only when no single party wins a majority and as the Congress emerged as the majority party the question of forging a coalition with the Muslim League did not arise. Jinnah, on the other hand, argued that coalition was the only respectable device to give to the Muslims a share in governing. Jawaharlal Nehru spurned Jinnah's demand ; and infuriated and humiliated, Jinnah directed from then onwards all his energy to keep the Muslims out of the Congress and assert his two-nation theory. It is arguable that a coalition at this time might have prevented Jinnah from intensifying his separatist demand.

In 1946 the Interim Government under the prime ministership of Jawaharlal Nehru was itself a coalition consisting of the Congress, the Muslim League, the Hindu Mahasabha, etc. The Congress Party, which has ruled India for so long, was until its split in 1969 itself consensual and coalitional in a sense keen as it always was to aggregate as many diverse viewpoints and ideoligies under its umbrella as practicable.

The credit of having the first-ever coalition under the present constitution goes to Pepsu.[3] As no party could muster a majority in the state assembly in the first general election of 1952 a coalition consisting of non-Congress parties (i.e. Akali Dal and others) was formed in April 1952. Lacking any ideological or programmatic homogeneity, the coalition barely lasted for eleven months and broke up in March 1953, followed by a spell of President's rule. The other states having coalition governments were Orissa, Andhra and Kerala. Significantly, all these coalitions were non-Congress ones. The Congress Party was the pre-eminent party dominating the political scene and having an absolutely majority of seats in the legislatures. Where a few exceptions occurred they were all coalitions (leaving aside Kerala in 1957-59) : perhaps, a necessary stage in party building in developing democracies.

The fourth general elections (1967) inaugurated an era of coalition governments in India in a big way. As many as eight states—Punjab, Haryana, U.P., Bihar, West Bengal, M.P., Orissa and Kerala—had coalition governments as a result of no party obtaining a majority of seats in the state legislatures. What should be further noted is that these states had coalition governments in quick succession : when one coalition fell another took over with marginal or substantial change in composition, depending on the local exigencies. It was a period of extreme political fluidity in the country. The monolith Congress Party failed to secure popular mandate, but no party emerged strong enough singly to replace it. In the event there occurred an apparently mindless rush for power, and the coalitions of this phase were generally in the nature of getting together of strange bed-fellows with the sole motivation of spiting the Congress and retaining political power in their hands. The mortality rate of such coalitions was bound to be very high.

Some governments were overtly coalitional consisting generally of multiplicity of parties. But there also arose the practice of minority government remaining in power with the support, but not active participation, of some other party. The only real difference between these two forms of government is that while all parties making coalition share both the responsibility and authority in it the party supporting

3. Patiala and East Punjab States Union was a Class B State until 1956 when it was merged with Punjab under the States Re-organisation Act.

the government from outside but not participating in it enjoys power without responsibility. Though called minority governments, they must be viewed as but a variant form of the coalition government. Minority governments were formed in Bihar, Punjab and West Bengal after the fourth general election. Invariably, such governments have proved to be singularly inept, ineffective and instable.

India, thus, became coalition-intensive after the general election of 1967. The Congress Party, which was the ruling party since the inauguration of the Constitution in 1950, returned to Lok Sabha with reduced majority and it no longer commanded an absolute majority in several states. This was a surprising development and a very uncomfortable one so far as the Congress was concerned. The defeat of the Congress in 1967 is a subject meriting some attention, and it is to this that one should turn one's attention.

The period between the third (1962) and fourth (1967) general election was an unusual one for India. It began with an armed conflict with China, and India was humiliated in this war. This turned the popular opinion against the ruling Congress party and even Jawaharlal Nehru's position suffered a measure of setback. Indeed Nehru's was the waning leadership from now onwards. At any rate Nehru passed away in 1964 and thus the Congress could no more count on his charismatic leadership. Even his successor, Lal Bahadur Shastri, did not live long enough to consolidate the position of the Congress Party. At the time of the 1967 general election the Congress Party had thus a leadership which could be broadly comparable to the leadership of any other major political party of the land : it no longer had any marked halo around it even though it had under its command a vastly superior organisational structure to fight the election.

Secondly, this period was of great economic hardship for India. The Third Five Year Plan had virtually come to a standstill. Besides, the country was overtaken by drought of a severe intensity. The national economy was thus sluggish and the country was passing through a period of acute inflation. In other words, the people were experiencing acute economic hardships and they were holding the Congress Party responsible for it.

Thirdly, the non-Congress Party had also begun to learn from their previous electoral mistakes. They gave up their earlier habit of contesting election separately thereby dividing the non-Congress votes, and thus pushing the Congress Party to victory. In the 1967 election the opposition parties developed the strategy of forming alliances thus preventing the splitting of votes as against the Congress. This surely paid them dividends, and the Congress was cut to its size. Besides, the opposition parties fielded their candidates in the election very selectively ; they generally concentrated in the constituencies where they felt reasonably sure of winning. This strategy paid them handsomely. The Congress, on the other hand, fought all the seats and thus spread itself over almost all the constituencies in the country. This surely increased the prospect of marginal losses for the party.

Fourthly, the plurality system of elections in vogue in India punished the Congress and rewarded the opposition parties in 1967 (as in 1977). The Congress lost more seats both in the Lok Sabha and the state assemblies than the votes. It barely polled 3.8 per cent less votes than in the last election to the Lok Sabha but lost 18.4 per cent seats (78 seats) ; similarly, it polled 4 per cent less votes than in the last election to the state assemblies but lost 12.2 per cent seats (337 seats).

The image of India being ruled by a single party has concealed the real dimensions of its coalitional politics. Since the inauguration of the Constitution in 1950, the country has witnessed no less than twenty eight coalitional governments in various states ; besides, the central government had a minority ministry during 1969-71 and coalition one during 1977-79. The split of 1969 in the Congress reduced the majority of Indira Gandhi's Congress which depended on the support of the DMK and the Communists. The Janata Government, in power from 1977 to 1979, was a coalition in a double sense. Though the Party was formed by the merger of the Congress (O), the BLD, the Jana Sangh, the Socialist Party and the Congress for Democracy, the constituent units never really ceased to exist within it and influence its functioning. Besides, it included the Akali Dal, thus fulfilling the criteria of a formal coalition. The states experiencing coalition since 1952 are Punjab, Haryana, U.P., Bihar, West Bengal, Orissa, M.P., Gujarat, Maharashtra, Karnataka, Tripura and Kerala. West Bengal, Kerala and, to an extent, Tripura have by now imbibed the coalitional culture, and a coalition in these states has come to be viewed as a normal political arrangement rather than an aberration. It is no small achievement that the CPI-led government in Kerala under Achuta Menon completed its full term ending March 1977. Equally stable is the leftist coalition in West Bengal under the chief ministership of Jyoti Basu. Coalition Governments are thus not a political abnormality in India. Even in 1984 Kerala, West Bengal, Karnataka and Tripura have each a coalition government.

Typology of coalition government

The coalition governments may be classified in many ways. This is because there are several variables which have a bearing on coalition making. A coalition may be a (i) dyadic coalition, (2) triadic coalition, or (iii) polyadic coalition. A dyadic coalition is an alignment of two separate groups of parties. The triadic and polyadic coalitions are alignments of three separate groups and more than two groups respectively. Coalitions may also be classified on the basis of the following questions :

1. What is the timing of the coalition making ?
2. What is the number of members in the coalition ?
3. What is the membership strength of the coalition members in relation to the total legislative membership ?
4. What are the ideologies of the members of coalition ?

One should take up these question one by one.

While discussing the timing of the coalition partners, a coalition may be either a pre-poll electoral alliance turning into a coalition government or a mere post-election coalition. From the point of view of number of members a coalition may be dyadic, triadic or polyadic. On the basis of the legislatve strength of the coalition members there may be a majority government coalition or a minority government coalition. Ideologically viewed a coalition may be homogeneous or heterogeneous. Further, even an ideologically homogeneous coalition may be (a) leftist, (b) rightist, (c) centrist or (d) neutral.

One may thus prepare the following Table 6.1. As this typology is derived from Indian political experience, examples are also mentioned in it.

TABLE 6.1 : **Typology of coalition government**

Basis of Classification	*Types*	*Example*
1. Timing	1. Pre-poll electoral alliance culminating into coalition government	Kerala after 1977 general election and 1970 mid-term poll ; West Bengal after the mid-term poll of 1969 and in 1972. West Bengal since 1977.
	2. Post-election governmental coalition	Coalition governments in U.P., Bihar, M.P., after 1967 election.

2. Number of parties	1. Dyadic	Congress (R)—BKD coalition in U.P. in 1970 and Swatantra—Jana Congress coalition in Orissa in 1970. Akali-Jana Sangh Coalition in Punjab.
	2. Triadic	Akali-Jana-Sangh-KMPP Coalition in Pepsu, 1952.
	3. Polyadic	Samyukta Vidhayak Dal Coalition in U.P., Bihar, M.P. after 1967 election, United Front coalitions in West Bengal.
3. Legislative Strength	1. Majority coalition government	Coalitions in West Bengal, M.P. U.P. etc. (Most coalitions fall in this type)
	2. Minority coalition government	P.C. Ghosh-led coalition in West Bengal in 1967-69, B.P. Mandal led coalition in Bihar in 1968 ; L.S. Gill led coalition in Punjab in 1968 ; Achuta Menon led ministry in Kerala in 1970.
4, Ideological Orientation	1. Ideologically homogeneous	Swatantra-Jana Congress coalition in Orissa, United leftist front government in West Bengal.
	2. Ideologically heterogeneous	SVD governments in UP, Bihar, M.P.. after 1967.
	3. Leftist coalition	United Leftist coalition in West Bengal.
	4. Rightst coalition	Swatantra-Jana Congress coalition in Orissa.
	5. Centrist coalition	Coaiition in Maharashtra in 1978.
	6. Ideologically neutral	Govind Narain Singh-led coalition governmeut in M.P. after 1967.

Multiplicity of parties

Coalition making becomes inescapable when there is a multiplicity of political parties contesting elections. A multi-party system may broadly be a result of two factors. Where the electoral system is based on proportional representation or list system, there is apt to be, as already indicated, a multiplicity of parties. France and Germany are the oft-quoted examples of such an electoral system producing a multy-party system. The second factor could be the pluralistic character of the society itself. The more the interests and viewpoints in the society competing for articulation, the more parties there are bound to be. Politics, broadly speaking, is a reflection of the society and a plural society seeks its echo in a multi-party system. Indian society shows continental diversities and differences with people living at varying levels of social, economic and cultural development. They, therefore, belong to different political groupings depending upon their own aspirations no less than their perception of interest. Thus viewed, the country is likely to have for a long time some five substantial parties. The biggest party may be a 'centrist' party and there may be two parties to the left and two to the right. One group of the left parties may consist of socialist parties and another the communist ones. One party on the right may accept democracy and secularism fully but may believe in free enterprise and more individual freedom in economic and fiscal matters. The other group of parties on the right may be traditionalist and believe in religious or cultural revivalism.

Though India is an example of one dominant party system it is characterised at the same time by a multiplicity of parties. The number of parties recognised by the Election Commission are shown in the following Table 6.2.

TABEE 6.2 : **Multiplicity of parties**

	1952	*1957*	*1962*	*1967*	*1971*	*1977*[4]	*1980*[5]
Number of National Parties	14	4	8	8	8	4	6
Number of Regional Parties	59	19	14	16	22	18	27

The multiplicity of parties has thus been viewed as a permanent feature of the political landscape of India, but this hardly posed any problem or concern in the system of governance. The Congress—which steered the country to Independence—was winning a majority of seats even though the votes polled in its favour never rose above 47.8 per cent for Lok Sabha and 42 per cent for state assemblies.

4. The Election Commission of India put the number of national parties at seven : Indian National Congress, Communist Party of India (Marxist), the Communist Party of India, Bhartiya Lok Dal, Indian National Congress (O), Bhartiya Jana Sangh and Socialist Party. The last-named four parties had formed the Janata Party in March 1977.
5. These are : the Congress (I), the Congress (U), the CPI, the CPM, the Janata Party, and Janata Party (S). The last one has since become the B.L.D.

The following Table 6.3 shows the percentage of votes secured by the ruling party since the first general election :

TABLE 6.3 : **Ruling parties in first general election**

S. No.	*Name of the Ruling Party*	*Year of Election*	*Percentage of Votes Obtained*
1.	Congress Party	1952	45
2.	Congress Party	1957	47.8
3.	Congress Party	1962	40.73
4.	Congress Party	1967	40.73
5.	Congress Party	1971	43.03
6.	Janata Party & Congress for Democracy	1977	43.17
7.	Congress Party	1980	42.58

The above pattern of voting discloses how close the country could be to a system of alliance goverance. A negative swing of a small margin is enough to knock the presently ruling Congress Party out of power. This apart, the opposition parties are increasingly seeking alliances and thus preventing the splitting of votes as against the Congress. But no other party seems to be in an immediate position singly to fill the gap thereby making a coalition government a near inevitability. Indeed, the one party dominant system appears to be on its way out, and its alternative, today, is an alliance system of governance. It may be safe to speculate that India will have to learn to live with coalitional arrangements for some time atleast before transiting into a two party system, even if this ever materialises. The coalition government is thus more than a political probability in India—at the Centre, and in the states. Kerala and West Bengal are already accustomed to this form. Punjab with Sikhs constituting 51 per cent of the population and Hindus 49 per cent would find in it the key to its political harmony.

Requisites for success of coalitions

Coalition governments in India have lasted for a few days but examples also exist of such alliances completing the full term of five years. This serves to prove that a coalition is not necessarily a highly vulnerable form of government even though it has shown the highest propensity for President's rule. The question then arises What factors make for the coalition logeveity ? A coalition made up of parties with a programme compatible with their ideologies is more durable than one which is unprincipled, formed purely for the sake of power. The coalition in Kerala is more stable precisely for this reason. So is the case with the United Front Government in West Bengal. Ideological homogeneity is thus a pre-requisite for the stability of a coalition. This gets further deepened if the coalition becomes an extension of the pre-election poll alliance as in West Bengal. On the other hand, when parties with differing political persuasions come together to form the government, the prospects of their staying together become dim. This may be illustrated by the case of Pepsu. In the general election of 1952 the party position in the Pepsu assembly was : Congress 16, Akali Dal 22, Jana Sangh 1, Commuuist Party 3, KMPP 1 and Independents 7, its total strength being 60. A coalition government of all the non-Congress parties was formed on 22 April 1952. The government consisted of highly disparate and divergent elements that they could not stay together for long, and it broke apart in less than a year. Similarly, an ideologically incompatible coalition consisting of parties like SSP, PSP, Jana Kranti Dal (later merged with BKD), and CPI was formed in Bihar in 1967 under the chief ministership of Mahamaya Prasad Sinha. It took office in March 1967 but fell in January 1968. The B.P. Mandal coalition in Bihar formed in February 1968 fell after 47 days precisely for this reason.

Another factor contributing to coalition stability is that it must find anchorage in a party which enjoys considerable strength in the legislature (Swatantra Party 49 in a House of 140 in Orissa in 1969 : Communist Party (Marxist) 52 in a House of 130 in Kerala in 1967). The inference is that where this kind of anchorage is not there, or is denied by the party capable of providing it, the coalitions will tend to be unstable. Hence, the denial of such an anchorage by a large party when with its support a stable government could have been formed places on it the responsibility for injuring the larger interests of state. Moreover, various parties in a coalition must have a fair distribution of power and patronage to deepen their sense of involvement in the government. But an excessive decentralisation too entails dangers for the coalition. L.P. Singh, the ex-governor of Assam, cites a case of this type.

> In one of the north eastern states a coalition cabinet of three regional parties functioned, in effect, as three sub-cabinets destroying the principle of joint responsibility and making adoption of a common policy or integrated administration impossible. The coalition had a short life.[6]

6. Ibid., p. 19.

A coalition government thus requires certain requisites for its success, but the role of the human factor is no less important. The human component of a coalition must be cultured and civilized; and imbued with a sense of purposeful service to the state.

7

POLITICAL FINANCE

POLITICS, like any other occupation, requires investment of capital to keep it going ; and if a society does not consciously provide for it, it manages to erupt in its own ways. Known also as 'money power in politics' or 'money power in election' the term 'political finance' is more expressive. 'Money power in politics' is not the same as 'money power in election'. The former is much more inclusive and the latter is a part of it. 'Money power in election' is a phenomenon seen only at the time of elections and is, moreover, sporadic. But money is used in a most intensive way to influence the outcome of an election in some preferred direction, and in the process it may even threaten to vulgarise this barometer of democracy and discredit the latter. A truly alarming development in the field of politics is the role which money power has come to play in elections. Each election is becoming more expensive than the preceding one, and the country does not seem to have reached a point of stability in this regard. The electoral laws of the land prescribe a ceiling on expenditure a candidate may incur, but the practice violates the law with the utmost impunity. Even the law has been distorted and vulgarised by amendments made in it around seventies. As a result, a distinction is drawn between the expenditure incurred by an aspiring candidate and that made by his party. The law ordains that an individual candidate must not spend more than the prescribed maximum, but is absolutely silent on the expenditure incurred by his party. This dichotomy is false and wicked and indeed makes a complete non sense of the election expense legislation.

It would be a sheer mental perversity to argue that money power has always played a crucial role in Indian politics. The role of money acquired gravity only when elections began to be held on the basis of adult franchise under the constitution.

Political finance under freedom movement

The Indian National Congress during the British period was basically the party of the masses under the charismatic leadership of

Mahatma Gandhi, and such of the political finance as was needed flowed essentially from small contributors. The methods of collection were highly symbolic and mobilisational in design, and in complete harmony with Indian culture and sentiments. The Congress used to raise its funds by one-anna and one-rupee subscriptions thus involving an ever increasing number of people. Similarly, after the paddy had been harvested, the party workers would collect a fistful of it from every farmer in the village thereby serving several ends simultaneously—gathering funds, socialising him in politics, broad-basing the participative process, etc. This manner of fund raising invoked the traditional sentiments of the people in a most powerful way and also, deepened popular commitment to the party. When people voluntarily make some contribution they tend also to show a measure of concern for the cause which it has set out to promote.

As political finance came from small contributors and the attempt always was to reach as large a number of people as possible there was felt no problem of money-power in the current usage of the term. This is because large donations were nearly non-existent even when the Congress Party came into power first under dyarchy and later under provincial autonomy. Donations sometimes were made in kind, particularly on certain special occasions but there was no reciprocity of thoughts much less guilty ones. For instance, it was a regular practice on the part of the Marwari Relief Society to make the catering arrangements for the members and delegates at the Congress annual sessions. It has been a part of the Indian philanthrophic traditions to support noble causes, and running of the Congress Party—perceived as a party of jail-goers—was one such activity. Similarly, it was common to look after the families of the freedom fighters with the Marwari money.

During the colonial period money had hardly any significant power in politics. It was an era of sacrifice-oriented politics and the entire ethos of the time was different. Moreover, the elections were not very regular and in any case were not held on universal franchise. With less number of voters the financial pressure on the party was much less, posing little problem.

A word may be said about other parties such as the Muslim League and the Communist Party. It is widely believed that the Muslim League used to get its fund—a substantial part of it—from the British Government and the Communist Party was regularly fuelled by 'foreign money'. This, at any rate, is the perception of many respectable Congressman whom the present author had interviewed.

Political finance since Independence

Independence changed the scenario in a fundamental way. The election of 1952 was the first election to be held on adult franchise, and the number of voters has been steadily increasing as is shown in the table below :

Number of voters

Years	*Number of Electorate*
1952	173 million
1957	193 ,,
1962	216 ,,
1967	250 ,,
1971	274 ,,
1977	321 ,,
1980	363 ,,

With the increasing number of electorate, the hitherto followed methods of political finance proved to be abortive, and new strategies in this respect had to be devised. Adult suffrage boosted the electoral expenses, and political finance became a subject of growing concern to the party managers. The arrangement devised at this time was that the contributions to the Congress fund were collected only by authorised persons at the central and the state levels, and through cheques. The general criteria governing the selection of the candidates was whether they could self-finance their election. The fourth general election held in 1967 saw the advent of new styles and strategies of campaign ; and the election of 1971 institutionalised and re-affirmed this new culture. The 1971 election is truly remarkable in India's electoral history from the standpoint of the political finance. The parliamentary and the state assembly elections were de-linked in 1971 for the first time in India, making it and each subsequent election very costly. Secondly, the criterion of selection of candidates underwent a change : it changed from financial viability of a candidate to his 'winnability'. In 1971 the percentage of self-financing candidates dropped to around twenty to twenty-five per cent only and the remaining ones looked inevitably to party funds to finance the election. This escalated the demand for party funds by the contesting candidates. The 1971 elections to Lok Sabha was the most expensive, and the Congress Party had collected colossal sums of money to contest it. It is guessed that atleast Rs. 20 crores were spent by in the 1971 Lok Sabha poll.

One must not overlook the environment in which such changes were taking place. The 1967 election constitutes a Great Divide in India's political history, for it signified coming to the forefront of new leadership in the country. Under the impact of these new forces the elections began to be fought on a much higher pitch, for they had to be won, *somehow*. The last words are significant : an election began to be viewed as a technicality which had to be completed—that is, won—*somehow*. Money and muscle power became mutually reinforcing, and both were fast getting integrated with election.

The political finance, as a result, became of critical importance for the Congress Party. It was no longer a party of small subscribers. In fact, today, the middle class contributes very little to the Congress—or to any other party. How is the finance, then, raised is an intriguing question. The present author interviewed a number of highly respectable members of the party, and what was communicated to him is accounted in what follows :

> The funds of the Congress Party have flowed from three main categories of persons. First, businessmen getting some favours of monetary importance have to portion with a portion of their potential profits in the form of party donations. For instance, we broadly know how much profit a certain licence is going to give to a bussinessman ; he is expected to donate to the party a percentage of the potential profit. Secondly, the Congress fund also flows on what may be called 'good will' basis. Here, no *quid-pro-quo* is involved, but certain industrial houses have been regularly making contributions to our funds because they have been our traditional friends. The third category includes those businessmen who do not want that our Party should be defeated at the hustings, for a political change may be harmful or ruinous to them. Hence, their support. The practice earlier was that funds for the party could be collected only by authorised persons and the party's treasurer was the repository of the funds. The situation has undergone a change now. There are now ministers who collect money ostensibly for party fund but it is never deposited. . . .

Estimates of poll expenses

An average Lok Sabha constituency of India has a population of nearly one million people of whom nearly 7 lakhs are voters. The state assembly constituency includes a population of about 1.5 lakh of whom about 80,000 are the voters. A voter is becoming growingly conscious of his rights and a candidate for office is expected to make a direct approach to the individual voter. Public meetings are organised ; posters and banners printed ; house-to-house canvassing undertaken ; transport hired ; and mass media harnessed. Each item costs money. 'Adversary politics' being vogue, the competitive spirit also tends to raise electoral expenses.

According to an Electoral Commission estimate made in 1980, a candidate for the Lok Sabha poll would be spending no less than Rs, 1.60 lakhs if he were only to hire three cars for a month, organise five public meetings, spend just Rs. 5,000 on posters, streamers, banners etc., keep the expenses on printing, paper and allowance to volunteers within moderate limits. This sum of Rs. 1.60 lakhs, one must note, is far above the revised ceiling law of Rs. 30,000.

This is a dated estimate today. A modestly contested parliamentary election would necessitate an expenditure of Rs. 5 lakhs, and an assembly one, rupees one lakh. One may then compute the election budget of a truly national political party, which would be of the order of over Rs. 60 crores. In a multi-party system the electoral expenses incurred by the parties would naturally be much higher. Electioneering is the biggest among the big business today ; a staggering sum of money is needed to keep it fuelled.

Contemporary profile of political finance

Money power in election has acquired several features, and one must take full note of them. In India, the election expenses are statutorily regulated—or at any rate, this was the practice originally. In seventies, however, a departure from such a stipulation was made and since then the statutory fixed ceiling of expenditure applies only to the expenses incurred by a candidate ; the funds spent by his political party or other supporting organisations are not the concern of the law. As a result, an individual candidate's expenditure on his election has all but lost importance ; and the party finance has assumed a serious role. The dependence on the party is on the increase, more so when the party happens to be the ruling one. Secondly, a definite shift in the source of political finance has occurred. The age of small subscribers is over, and today, the parties are maintained—that is, funded—by big business houses. This was confessed even by Government as early as in 1959. Lal Bahadur Shastri, the then central minister for commerce and industry, observed in 1959 while speaking on the Companies (Amendment) Bill, 1959[1] : "Individuals these days make very little political contri-

1. *Lok Sabha Debates*, Second Series Twelfth Session, Vol. XLVIII, No 12, 29 November, 1960, Col. 2866,

butions." Until 1959 the companies could lawfully make any amount of contributions to political parties. In 1959 the upper limit of contribution was fixed at Rs. 25000, which was the ceiling of expenditure for a parliamentary election at that time. Since 1969 there is a total ban on political contributions by companies. The legal provisions however, have no applicability. The company donations are, today, the mainstay of political parties. When parties have reached a stage when they require crores of rupees to contest elections the original provision for the upper limit of Rs. 25,000 was ridiculously low, and a total ban is purely hypocritical. Indeed, the restrictive provision relating to political finance by companies has given rise to the problem of what is known as parallel economy and political corruption. The business houses make or are made to make—large scale political contibutions clandestinely—in cash and without showing these in their account books. The whole transaction is vitiated and vicious, being the direct instigator and absorber, of corruption.

As already emphasized, a shift in the source of political finance from individual subscribers to companies occurred in the early years of Independence. Of late, a further shift is seen from individual companies to their federating organisations. The ruling party, for instance, collects the funds from the Indian Sugar Manufacturers' Association (ISMA) rather than from individual sugar mills : the innovation is time-saving and conducive to efficiency. This is true of many other sectors of industry also. Politics, today, needs billions of rupees to sustain itself, and the fund-raisers find it more convenient to negotiate with the collective organisation rather than with individual units. This is the third attribute of political finance in India.

Fourthly, the fund-raisers themselves have changed over a period time. Historically, the party was collecting funds, but of late there is a definite swing from the party to the Government. What this implies is that while in the past the political funds were raised by those on the organisation wing of the Party the onus has now shifted to the ministerial wing. This itself is reflective of a subtle but fundamental change in the political and social values of the larger community. The president of a state level Congress committee may today find it beyond his capacity to collect even one lakh rupees, but even a deputy minister in the Government may collect crores of rupees quickly and noiselessly. This stands in sharp contrast to the practice of the early days when men like C.B. Gupta (U.P.) could collect the party funds without much difficulty even though he was on the organisation side of the party. People had natural respect for the political leaders at that time, but today donations are given to a minister because of the power and authority which he commands.

Finally, the emergence of multi-national corporations have changed the character of political finance in a perceptible way and added new dimensions to it. The multi-national corporations are fast integrating themselves with the national economy,—and perhaps politics—of the host country and their work style have triggered off changes in many areas of the country's public life. As a rule, these companies regularly and religiously keep a fund which is spent as 'consideration' for securing contracts and other favours. The widely publicised Lockheed deal is a normal work-pattern of MNCs in India as perhaps in many other countries. There is a 'kick back' money given to the designated individuals for every order that is secured from the government, the amount depending upon the size of the favour secured. Indeed, the MNCs are fast emerging as the principal financiers of parties, particularly of the ruling party in the country. The 'kick back' money is either deposited in foreign banks or handed over to the designated persons.

Finally, cleanliness in political donations has completely vanished, and today the field of political finance is seething with corruption. Earlier, the regular practice of the companies was to make political contributions exclusively through cheques to only authorized persons like the party treasurer or president. Men like C.B. Gupta were most meticulous and honest in this regard never collecting any contribution in cash and letting it diverted for personal use : all such collections were most scrupulously deposited in the party account. Today, the donations are in the form of cash, and there is no restriction on the number of those 'authorised' to collect party funds. As a result, all on the ministerial side of the Government collect the party funds, and what is deposited in the party's account and what is retained by the fund collector is generally left to his own value system, although the head of the Government is reported to be keeping such fund-mobilisers under a general surveillance to prevent excessive privatisation.

The Congress leadership under Jawaharlal Nehru did not involve the career civil service in fund collection even though the base of political finance had emphatically shifted from the organisational wing to the ministerial one. Civil servants were for the first time used for raising political finance after the fourth general election (1967) and what is more, the move in this direction came from the Samyukta Vidhayak Dals—those loose coalitions consisting of the non-Congress parties. The SVD Governments, as we all know, were made up of parties not very well organised and moreover, were entirely new to the job of ruling. Their contacts with potential financiers, too, were necessarily limited. They, therefore, had virtually no option but to lean on the shoulders of the civil servants and involve them in the business of funds-raising. The constituent parties were not homogeneous and were riven by feelings of mutual mistrust which too, kept them apart from each other. The minister responsible for sugarcane development, to cite a hypothetical example, might have entrusted the task of raising political finance with the cane commissioner, a bureaucrat. Similarly, the excise commissioner in the state was generally asked by his minister to collect funds for his party. It is in this way that the civil service began to be used for political finance. Since those days of the SVDs, the various governments, both Congress and non-Congress, do not much hesitate in utilising the civil servants for fund-raising purposes. But one must note that they, exercising as they do direct power and authority, may collect fund from their clientele but their capacity in this regard is limited in terms of the need for political finance. 'They can at best manage lakhs of rupees, not crores which are needed by the parties today', said one repondent. As such the parties cannot rely only on this agency for their financial requirements.

The various advantages referred to above are available in all their amplitude to the party which is in the seat of power, more so at the centrol level. The question of how the opposition parties raise their finance need also to be examined. 'Opposition' is a relational role ; and on a closer analysis it will be found that a party in opposition at the centre may be a ruling one at the state level. This is indeed the case in India today. The Communist Party, the Janata Party, the Telegu Desam, the AIADMK, the National Conference etc. are all ruling parties in some state or the other. In its role of a ruling party, it cashes all the advantages which, for instance, the Congress Party does at the central level—with much extended scope, of course. The state governments are also awarding contracts and orders to industrialists and to multi-national corporations. Even otherwise, wherever public expenditure is involved there is always an opportunity to 'privatise' atleast a part of it. The opposition parties are thus not completely destitute of resources, although their capacity to raise fund is limited because of their rule.

Company donations to parties

The company legislation in India was amended in 1959 to provide for limited company donations to political parties, the maximum contribution being fixed at five per cent of the profit in a year or Rs. 25,000 which ever being more.

The legal sanction for company donations, even though subject to a ceiling, was deeply offensive to the saintly image of Indian politics, and the Committee on Prevention of Corruption under K. Santhanam (1964) discouraged the practice in emphatic terms. It made three suggestions in this regard. First, the ban on company donations should be extended to include all kinds of direct and indirect contributions including souvenirs, advertisements etc. Secondly, the funds of the various parties should be brought under the control of the law and the Election Commission should appoint auditors and publish their account books. Thirdly, limits should be prescribed for political parties together with their respective candidatess and these must be enforced strictly.

In 1969 a total ban on company donations was imposed, apparently in a bid to curb corruption. It was argued in the process of amendment of the necessary law that such donations corrupted public life and thus adversely affected the wholesome development of democracy. The ban on company donation continues, but is honoured only in its undisguised breach. This is because the law itself is studded with exemptions thereby diluting its coverage. But this is only a smaller part of its weakness. Its failure lies in the fact that the politicians who enacted it in all its severity are themselves not willing to abide by its provisions. In practice huge sums of money continue to flow into the coffers of the political parties. The Congress Party in March 1977 had collected Rs. 8 crores from companies in the form of payments for advertisements in the party souvenirs[2]. A businessman is understandably anxious to be on the right side of the Government which is committed to planning and mixed economy, for his survival under such a system depends upon the goodwill of the ruling party. The companies, therefore, allow themselves to be coerced by the ruling party into contributing large sums of money to the party coffers. As donations are banned under the law, they are made in cash, and as such no receipts are given. Nor are payments shown in account books. It is anybody's guess how much of this secret money is

2. *The Times of India*, 6 September 1977,

paid into the party kitty and how much is retained for personal benefit. It is said that ministers both at the central and the state levels make crores of rupees for their personal benefit in the process of party fund collection.

The payment of money to party funds is the major cause of corruption in the country. It is plainly based on *quid pro quo* ; and, as Lal Bahadur Shastri asserted in 1959, corrupts both the giver to the donations and the receiver of it. Once a person gets a taste of getting money, even though for election funds, he would be inclined to indulge in it again and again and demand more and more. The resultant losses the industrialists would seek to recoup by questionable methods. How they cleanse the Augean stables is a question which defies a solution in India.

The Electoral Reforms Committee which Jayaprakash Narayan had appointed in the seventies recommended that the ban on business companies should continue. It wrote :

> We are not satisfied that legalising company donations will necessarily prevent clandestine payments being extorted from companies and we, therefore, recommend that the present ban on corporate donations should continue. Indeed, we believe that the way in which the ban at present is being evaded by large payments being made for so-called advertisements in the so-called souvenirs of political parties should be prevented by law.[3]

The Government does not intend to withdraw restrictions on company donations to politlcal parties. This was the reply to a question tabled in the Rajya Sabha on 1 March 1982. Donations by companies to political parties, presently banned by law, should be restored to control the effects of black money on the country's economy. The reason why company donations should be allowed was best explained in 1959 when the Companies Act was amended to legalise limited political contributions. Lal Bahadur Shastri, the then Minister for Commerce and Industry, defended giving of donations, and observed :

> Individuals these days make very little political contributions because they say there are heavy taxes and if what they contribute is taxable they are not prepared to make any contributions. The

3. See *Indian Express*, 26 November 1974.

> result will be (that) these people will give contributions and somehow manage that money comes out of the company funds. There will be taking of accounts and I do not think that Acharyaji or Shri Masani (who were opposing this provision) would like to allow subterfuge methods to be adopted for making contributions from the profits of the company in some form or the other. If the Honourable Members face realities they will see that we prevent that kind of manipulation, etc. if we provide this clause here. If manipulation of funds is made, it will demoralise those who give and also those who take it.[4]

The ban on party donations must be withdrawn, and at the same time other measures are necessary. It must be made obligatory for political parties to register themselves with the Election Commission and maintain their accounts. Such a legislation is already in force in USA and the Federal Republic of Germany. This would be conducive to the healthy growth of party system in India. Donations to political parties should be made only through crossed cheques. Moreover, the accounts of all political parties and candidates should be audited by independent auditors appointed by the Election Commission, and such audited accounts should be made public.

Foreign money

A discussion of political finance in India is apt to remain incomplete without a discussion, even though brief, of the role which the 'foreign money' is playing. It is a most tricky topic, for it is admittedly impossible to prove cnnclusively whether foreign money flows into India to manipulate politics and further to identify its recipients. The present author discussed this issue with several distinguished persons, and what is related here is based strictly on these interview records.

Foreign money, largely American and Russian, but also Gulf and European, has been flowing into India for quite a long time notwithstanding the existence on the statute book of the Foreign Contribution (Regulation) Act, 1976 which prohibits acceptance of foreign money or hospitality without the Government's permission. The geo-political importance of India has evoked the interest of many foreign countries in its political institutions and processes. Injection of foreign money is a part of these countries' global

4. *Lok Sabha Debates*, Twelfth Session, Vol. XLVIII, Col. 2866.

strategy to manipulate the course of governmental action to their favour and to destabilise the established regimes. The Soviet funds have remained available to the Communist Party in India since the year of its inception in 1928 and the British Government in India was subsidising the Muslim League. The inflow of foreign money has been increasing over a period of time. A few years ago, the former U.S. Ambassador to India, Daniel Patrick Moynihan, disclosed that the U.S. Embassy in Delhi had doled out grants to certain political leaders in India. Many public organisations have become conduits for flow of foreign money into India. The Gulf money, for instance, is pouring into the country for promoting Islam, and the recent Harijans' mass conversions to Islam is directly related to its influx. The Christian missionaries in the North-Eastern India are not devoid of political interests and are arousing disquieting thoughts. The socialist parties in the country have been receiving funds from socialist movements in Europe. The Soviet Union and other East European countries deal directly with private traders in India, and the 'kick backs' and commissions given to private traders are used, it is believed, for financing selected political parties. Some members of political parties and pressure groups maintain contacts with foreign embassies in Delhi and cash is gushing into Indian hands in copious quantity. Some diplomatic missions patronise certain newspapers with large paid advertisements and thus influence public opinion. The foreign money is fuelled into Indian politics in many subtle and sophisticated ways. One form of it is through advertisements in mass media. One may thus see a foreign country inserting full-page advertisements in selected newspapers and souvenirs and thus foreign funds get injected into the country. Foreign money flows also in the form of local currency. Some time ago, Indian rupees were being bought in huge quantities in Abu Dhabi and such other places and the money was later clandestinely pumped into India, it is said, by the Soviet Union, the Communist Party and its splinters being the direct beneficiaries. Likewise, the CIA money is flowing, among others, to some political parties, especially to the regional parties including the parties in the north-eastern region. It is even alleged that the Bhartiya Janata Party itself is a recipient of CIA benefits. It seems, Indian politicial parties have reached a stage of accommodation and compromises that they all are guilty of some transgressions or the other. Most of them are beneficiaries of foreign money, some more, some less. This view receives reinforcement and confirmation from the life-style which many politicians regardless of their party affiliations lead.

Problems and issues

The legitimacy of the election gets seriously eroded if entry into it becomes unequal, and one factor which works for such a state is the money power. It is indeed to curb the money powers that the state has enacted specific legislation requiring each candidate to keep his election expenses within the prescribed limit. The statutory intervention to control expenses on election seeks to equalise opportunities to contest and win elections—to enable, in other words, even a candidate with moderate means to seek public office.

The growing role of money power in eleclions thrwarts the democratic process in many ways. It effectively prevents people with modest means from contesting, and thus the polity becomes plutocracy and narrow-based with all attendant consequences. The contesting candidates are ever on the look out for those who command the necessary resources and in the process compromises and understandings are reached to the detriment of the larger public interest. Those having monetary resources thus acquire political power posing a direct threat to democracy. It is in this context that a parallel economy based on black money has come to exist in India—an aspect which has been discussed in the chapter on 'Political Corruption.'

Electoral reform is absolutely essential in the interest of purity in public life in India. Rightly did President V.V. Giri warn the nation in his 1974 Independence Day eve message :

> It has been a most regrettable development in recent years that money power has come to play such a dominant role in the elections to legislatures. This to my mind is at the root of corruption and corrupt influences in our public life.[5]

The Chief Election Commissioner of India has made a number of recommendations for electoral reform which ought to be given serious and early attention. In a bid to reduce dependence on money-power, he has proposed the setting up of a Rs. 100 crore electoral fund whereby elections would be financed by the State. All political parties are generating and using unaccounted money at present, which would be reduced with the adoption of the above proposal.

The State may institute a fund partially to finance elections. The money earmarked for the State Fund should be allotted, as

5. *The Statesman*, 15 August 1974.

in West Germany and Scandinavian countries, on the basis of the proportion of votes polled by each party with the lower limit of say 3 to 5 per cent of the votes polled. Parties receiving less than this percentage should not be eligible for aid. This aid could cover such items as free supply of electoral rolls to recognised parties, provision of wherewithal for issue of identity slips etc. As R.K. Trivedi, the Chief Election Commissioner of India, rightly warns, no direct cash subsidy for meeting election expenditure should be given to the political parties.[6] Equally necessary is the reform of political parties of the land. In West Germany the Constitution obliges each political party to 'publicly account for the sources of their funds'. In India how the political finance is raised and managed is not made public, which is a highly anachronistic situation. Where the political finance of Himalayan magnitude is involed, it must allow itself to be regulated under a comprehensive law of the land.

6. R.K. Trivedi's keynote address at the Institute of Constitutional and Parliamentary Studies on 27 March 1983.

8

POLITICAL ENQUIRIES

THE INQUISITORIAL functions of a modern state are becoming progressively important which is borne out by the appointment of an increasing number of inquiry commissions. India is no exception to this phenomenon. The inquiry bodies are brought into being to serve a wide variety of purposes. Policy-making evidently requires a viable data-base, but there may understandably be many areas where the necessary information is not already in the possession of the government, at least in the quantity and form desired, and in such a context the appointment of an inquiry commission for intelligence-gathering becomes essential for sound public policy-making. Today, the governments in the Third World—and elsewhere also—find themselves enlarging their tasks and moving into areas impinging on the social, economic and cultural activities of the people, the underlying urge being to regulate, to promote, or even to manage them. As such, far more occasions present themselves for the appointment of such inquiry commissions. Secondly, the political system is not entirely immune to malpractices and maladministration ; things sometime go wrong and failures or inadequacies in policies or which is more common, their executions are noticed. The society as well as the government are naturally anxious to find out why the lapses occurred, and an examination becomes necessary to affix the fault, identify those responsible for it and, what is most important, suggest corrective measures for the future. Thirdly, an inquiry commission is also preferred to study, objectively and dispassionately, some currently controversial problems and determine the facts, a task which is at once delicate and important when some public issues become politically charged and even threaten to divide the nation. Sir Cyril Salmon, Lord Justice of Appeal in Great Britain, observed while delivering a talk on 'Tribunals of Inquiry' :

> In all countries, certainly in those which enjoy freedom of speech and a free press, moments occur when allegations and rumours

> cirulate causing a nation-wide crisis of confidence in the integrity of public life or about other matters of vital public importance No doubt this rarely happens, but when it does it is essential that public confidence should be restored, for without it no democracy can long survive. This confidence can be effectively restored only by thoroughly investigating and probing the rumours and allega tions so as to search out and establish the truth. The truth may show that the evil exists, thus enabling it to be rooted out, or that there is no foundation in the rumours and allegations by which the public has been disturbed. In either case, confidence is restored.[1]

These commissions when appointed have to collect the information on matters falling within the scope of their investigation and to this end they take evidence of the witnesses, scrutinise papers and documents, both governmental and non-governmental, and sometimes even conduct their own researches to fill the gaps. In order to ensure the availability of all necesary papers as well as the presence of witnesses, these bodies require to be clothed with powers similar to those enjoyed by the ordinary courts of law. It is precisely this purpose which is subserved by the Commissions of Inquiry Act, which the Indian Parliament enacted in 1952.

Genesis of the Commissions of Inquiry Act

Before the passing of this Act, the data-base of such commissions as were appointed rested on the will of others to give evidence and make available the necessary documents. Appearance of witnesses before a commission for tendering evidence and submission of necessary documents was voluntary, for legally speaking it could not compel compliance with its behests The whole arrangement cf intelligence gathering was weak and unorganised. It is true that if a particular commission felt it necessary to have certain witnesses or papers it sought the powers of a judicial court and if the Government agreed, it enacted a special law for it. Indeed it was a somewhat regular practice for the government to enact a legislation giving this kind of powers to an investigating body, But this device was time-consuming. The limitations of the current practice were becoming increasingly frustrating, and when in 1950 the Sugar Inquiry Committee, appointed under the chairmanship of Justice Ganga Nath,

1. Salmon, Sir Cyril : *Tribunals of Inquiry*, Jerusalem, The Habrew University, 1967, p. 5.

to look into the sugar crisis of 1949 began its work it felt not inconsiderably handicapped in its task. This Committee pinpointed a need for invesitng inquiry bodies with the necessary powers to summon notes and documents as well as witnesses. The Sugar Inquiry Committee on the Sugar Crisis of July-August 1949, which is the nomenclature of this body, observed.

> "... the Committee started its work on the assumption that it would get full cooperation from the public, industry, and trade on a voluntary basis. The difficulties of doing so, however, become apparent when the Committee received letter No. OMS/1008/Sugar dated 11 July 1950 from the Manager, E.I.R....in which it was stated :
>
> Efforts were made to collect particulars of the actual consignees from the Mills but the Mills regretted their inability to supply this information on the plea that it was "off - season" for them and they did not have the necessary staff to providc this information.
>
> The Committee at once informed the Government of India and wrote that the Committee should have powers to collect evidence and information necessary to deal with points to be enquired into and that if it waited for further evidence of failure to obtain information on a voluntary basis, it was apprehended that the proceedings of the inquiry might be unduly delayed. The fears of the Committee were confirmed when the time given for statements of views on the points under enquiry and names of persons who would like to givc evidence and replies to the questionnaires expired on 20 July and 25 July (1950) respectively. The Committee again wrote to the Government and informed it of the poor and discouraging response from the public, trade and industry. To remedy the matters, Sugar Crisis Enquiring Authority Ordinance No. XXV of 1940 ... giving necessary powers to the Committee was promulgated on 1 September 1950."[2]

The Central Government, thereupon, decided to enact a general legislation which would have the effect of putting the inquiry commissions on a par with courts of law in the matter of empowering the commissions to summon the necessary documents and witnesses. The legislation bears the nomenclature of the Commissions of Inquiry Act, 1952.

2. *Report of the Sugar Inquiry Committee on the Sugar Crisis of July- August 1949*, Delhi, Manager of Publications, 1951, pp. 2-3.

The Commissions of Inquiry Act, 1952 was modelled on the Tribunal of Inquiry (Evidence) Act, 1921 of Great Britain. Before the enactment of this statute in Great Britain there was the practice of Select Parliamentary Committees to investigate the alleged wrong-doing in high places. No wonder, such a probe usually toed the party lines, and ministers apparently felt secure behind the party majority in the House of Commons even though they might have been guilty of misconduct[3]. It was precisely to displace such a partisan style of inquiring into cases of misconduct that the British Parliament was induced to enact the Tribunal of Inquiry (Evidence) Act, 1921.

Constitution and the 'Probe' function

It is good to recall at this stage that item 94 in the union list of the Constitution refers to "inquiries, surveys and statistics for purposes of any of the matter in this list." Likewise, item 45 in the concurrent list relates to "inquiries and statistics for the purposes of any of the matters specified in list II or list III"[4] and thus empowers both the Central government and the state governments to appoint commissions on matters which have been placed within the exclusive jurisdiction of the states as well as on those concurrently within the jurisdiction of both the Centre and the states. "The power of the union government is, of course, wide. It covers the entire field. It covers the exclusive union field under list I and is expressly authorised to appoint committees in relation to list II also, namely the state sphere. On the other hand, the state government can only appoint committees and commissions in relation to its own sphere."[5]

Enactment of the Commissions of Inquiry Bill

The Commissions of Inquiry Bill was introduced in the House of the People (as was the Lok Sabha called at that time) on 11 July 1952 and the same day it was referred to a Select Committee which was asked to report back in ten days' time. On 27 July 1952, the Lower House considered the Bill as reported by the Select Committee and passed it. This Act was put into force on 1 October 1952 and has

3. Salmon, Sir Cyril : *Tribunals of Inquiry*, *op. cit*, p. 6.
4. It may be mentioned that list I is the union list, list II the state one, and list III is the concurrent one.
5. The observation made by K.N. Katju, then Home Minister, while moving the Commissions of Inquiry Bill in the Lok Sabha. *Parliamentary Debates-House of the People*, Part II, Vol. III, No. 6, 11 July 1952, Vol. 3633.

been since in operation in its original form exeept for a minor amendment introduced in 1971.

The Bill did not encounter any marked opposition in the Parliament, but a few critical observations made in the course of the debate may be noted here. As it was intended to be standing piece of legislation applicable to all inquiry commissions, one member had his misgivings and even expressed his preference for the *status quo ante* under which the Government was obliged to come to Parliament every time it was to constitute a commission of inquiry and thus to justify its action to the satisfaction of the people's representatives. This meant better accountability.

> The first question which we should like to ask the Honourable Home Minister is whether *ad hoc* legislation would not have been better. Whenever we introduce *ad hoc* legislation before a particular House for constituting a commission of inquiry, we have to make out the grounds for constituting such a commission of inquiry. We have to find out 'public interest'. The House would be in a better position to review the whole question of public interest and would really be in a better position to clothe this commission with such powers.[6]

Two speakers perceived an infringement of the states' autonomy by empowering New Delhi to set up probe bodies on subjects within the state list of the constitution. M.S. Gurupadaswamy, a Member from (old) Mysore, pointed out : ". . . The present Bill seeks to encroach upon even the minimum subjects that have been handed over to the state governments. It seeks to set up commissions of inquiry into matters relating to subjects which come under the state list. I submit that this is nothing but an infringement upon the minimum autonomy that is given to or the minimum independence that is being enjoyed by many of the states, and that the central government or the Hon. Mintster has not taken the opinion of the (state) governments concerned with regard to this matter."

He went on to remark that "the draftsman in the central secretariat has just drafted the Bill and it has been submitted to Parliament without reference to anybody."[7] He alleged that instead of facilitating

6. Krishnaswami's speech in the House of People, *Parliamentary Debates-House of the People*, Part II, Vol. III, No. 6, col. 3654
7. *Parliamentary Debates-House of the People*, Part II, Vol. III, No. 19, 29 July 1952, col. 4780,

the smooth functioning of administration, the bill contained within itself the seeds of bitterness and friction between the centre and the states. Vallatharas, another Member of Parliament, commented.

> . . . I stoutly oppose the encroachment upon state subjects in list II...The dignity of the Central government requires that it should confine itself to great matters of policy such as the safety of the state, and not to smaller matters which are absolutely the concern of the states to control by local legislation.[8]

It is no less instructive to infer from the general tenor of the parliamentary discussion that this legislation was intended to apply to such inquiries as related to social or economic problems, or to matters of importance to the welfare of the people such, for example, as land reforms. Besides, some issues are inevitably of concern to more than one state, and in such cases the central government was better suited to institute a commission of inquiry empowered to investigate the problem in its entirety unhampered by individual state boundaries. Venkataraman dilated upon the many uses of inquiries while supporting this measure in the House :

> Let us look at the cases in which such enquiries are usually ordered. They are matters of utmost social importance. It is not against any individual person that a commission of inquiry has ever been appointed. To my knowledge I do not know if ever a committee or a commission of inquiry was appointed to inquire into the conduct of a person. The commission of inquiry is usually appointed to go into some matter of social importance like the sugar industry or say for instance an inquiry into the conditions of working in certain industries, in plantations and so on and so forth. So in these matters if the commissions are prevented from going into the root of the matter and trying to find out the real conditions in that industry, we shall have to be content with only what the other side gives as their (sic.) version.[9]

K.N. Katju, the Home Minister, refuted all the charges made by the critics. According to him, neither was this legislation to cause any abridgement of the states' autonomy nor was the central government

8. Ibid, col. 4789.
9. *Parliamentary Debates-House of the People*, Part II, Vol. III, No. 6, col. 3660.

intending to invoke it unilaterally, that is, without a process of consultation with the state concerned. While replying to the debate, he observed :

> On this question of interference with (state) autonomy, I would ask the House to consider that the commission of inquiry is a purely advisory body. It has got no powers and cannot have any powers, either executive or legislative. The function of the commission of inquiry is to find facts and to make recommendations. If it is a matter exclusively in the state list, then it will be upon the state concerned to take appropriate action. But there may be numerous cases in which fact-finding investigation may be necessary in the interest of the state itself...No central government will act unless it be in the closest collaboration with the state government concerned.

He further emphasized:

> We must attribute some sense, some common sense, some reasonableness to all governments, and not just say that autonomy is being interferred with because the matter is in list II and, therefore, should remain sacrosanct and should not be touched.[10]

Principal provisions of the Act

Either level of government in India can appoint a commission to inquire into 'any definite matter of public importance.',[11] and must do so if the legislature passes a resolution in favour of setting up such a body to examine some specified matter. While the state government is empowered to have probes ordered only on subjects within its own sphere of functions or the sphere concurrently common to both the centre and the states, the centre government's writ, in this respect, runs over all the three lists in the constitution's seventh schedule. The statute provides that the inquiry commission may consist of one or more members appointed by the appropriate government, and where it has more than one member, one of them is appointed as its chairman. It is clothed with all the powers and facilities normally enjoyed by the courts of law in the country. It can, for instance, summon and enforce the attendance of any person and

10. *Parliamentary Debates-House of the People*, Part II, Vol. III, No. 19, 20 July 1952, col 4795.
11. Section 3 (1) the Commissions of Inquiry Act, 1952,

examine him on oath, require the production of any documents, receive evidence on affidavits, examine any witnesses, and the like.

Use of the Commissions of Inquiry Act

The Commissions of Inquiry Act, 1952 has been invoked for inquiries of various kinds and by both the levels of Government, and by 1977 nearly 200 commissions have been set up. The Central government itself has pressed it into service when instituting commissions to inquire into problems in the fields of social, economic and political affairs. Commissions have been appointed to look into wide-ranging subjects such as police firings, contamination of river waters, dam bursts, management of religious institutions, assassination of political leaders, etc. Some inquiry commissions have been set up to look into certain instances of malpractices also, an example being the Committee of Inquiry (Steel Transactions) set up by the Central government in 1966, its chairman being A.K. Sarkar. Similarly in November 1979, the Madhya Pradesh Government appointed a commission under the chairmanship of Justice R.J. Bhave to inquire into irregularities in the grant of *gulabi* gram export permits, collection of funds for scarcity relief in Damoh district, and the purchase of jute matting.

There have also been inquiry commissions in the field of public administration. The Second Pay Commission (1959-60) and the Third Pay Commission (1973) were bodies set up under the Commissions of Inquiry Act, 1952. The Chagla Inquiry Commission appointed to look into certain dealings of the Life Insurance Corporation (1958) was also of the same piece. It need be noted here that all these commissions were set up to inquire into some specific problems of significant public importance ; and individuals as such were not made the object of any examination.

But it did not take the Centre—and later the states—long to discover new uses of this statute. The year 1964 witnessed the first-ever use of the Commissions of Inquiry Act for examining charges of corruption against the members of political executive and by the eighties there have been nineteen instances of this kind. Surprisingly, all such commissions have been appointed against the ministers in the states, no central minister having been subjected to a probe by such a body during the thirty-year uninterrupted rule by the Congress Party. It was under the Janata Party rule (1977-79) that commissions against some former central government ministers were appointed. What is more, the inquiry commissions against the state level ministers have been set up by both the central government and the state governments.

The centre has been ordering probes against the state ministers while still continuing in office or as in the case of Karunanidhi, immediately after dismissing the ministry on charges of corruption. Of the four cases one chief minister belonged to the ruling party at the Centre while the remaining three came from other parties. A state government has been generally setting up inquiry bodies against the members of the previous ministry belonging to a different political party or a coalition. The following is the list of such commissions set up by various governments from time to time[12] :

Central Government

Name	*Year of Appointment*	*Year of Submission of Report*
1. The Commission of Inquiry against Pratap Singh Kairon, the chief minister of Punjab (Chairman : S.R. Das)	1963	1964
2. The Commission of Inquiry against M. Karunanidhi the ex-chief minister of Tamil Nadu, and some other ex-ministers (Chairman : R.S. Sarkaria)	1976	1978
3. The Commission of Inquiry against Vengal Rao, the Chief Minister of Andhra Pradesh, and some other ministers (Chairman : J.R. Vimadalal)	1977	1979
4. The Commission of Inquiry against Devaraj Urs, the Chief Minister of Karnataka, and some other ministers (Chairman : A.N. Grover)	1977	1978
5. The Commission of Inquiry into the allegations against certain former ministers of Punjab (Chairman : L.N. Chhangani)	1971	1975

12. After the June 1977 assembly poll several State Governments controlled by the non-Congress Party or parties announced inquiry commissions against the ministers in the previous Congress government. These states are Himachal Pradesh, Madhya Pradesh, Punjab, and West Bengal, Karnataka, though under the Congress rule, set up an inquiry commission against some existing members as well as those in the preceding state ministries. All these commissions proved to be infructuous.

Name	Year of Appointment	Year of submissions of Report
6. The Commission of Inquiry regarding Bansilal (chairman : P. Jaganmohan Reddy)	1977 —	1979
STATES		
Bihar		
1. The Commission of Inquiry against K.B. Sahay and other ex-ministers (Chairman : T.L. Venkatarama Aiyar)	1967	1970
2. The Commission of Inquiry against Mahamaya Prasad Sinha and other ex-ministers (Dhairman : Mudholkar)	1968	1970
Jammu and Kashmir		
1. The Commission of Inquiry against Bakshi Ghulam Mohammed (Chairman : N. Rajagopalan Ayyangar)	1965	1967
Orissa		
1. The Commission of Inquiry against Biju Patnaik and other 14 ministers, (Chairman : H.R. Khanna)		1967
2. The Commission of Inquiry against Harekrishana Mehtab (Chairman : Sarjoo Prasad)	1971	1972
3. The Commission of Inquiry to look into Kendu Leaf Purchases (Chairman : G.K. Mitter)	1973	1974
Kerala		
1. The Commission of Inquiry against K.R. Gouri (Chairman : S. Vellu Pillai)	1969	1971
2. The Commission of Inquiry against E.K. Imbichi Bava (Chairman : S. Vellu Pillai)	1969	1971
3. The Commission of Inquiry against M.K. Krishnan (Chairman : S. Vellu Pillai)	1969	1970
4. The Commission of Inquiry against P.R. Kurup (Chairman : S. Vellu Pillai)	1971	1972

Name	*Year of Appointment*	*Year of Submission of Report*
5. The Commission of Inquiry against Govindan Nair and T.V. Thomas (Chairman : A.N. Mulla)	1969	1971
6. The Commission of Inquiry against B. Wellington (Chairman : P. Govindan Menon)	1970	1972
7. The Commission of Inquiry against P.K. Kunju (Chairman : S. Vellu Pillai)	1970	1971

Procedure for determining and conducting an inquiry

The procedure which the eentral government has evolved for processing the complaints against ministers is that, when a memorandum against a political executive is submitted, it—provided it has a political inclination to pursue the issue—forwards it to the latter and seeks his comments. These comments are then examined by the Centre and if it finds a prima facie case it announces an inquiry commission. The present procedure is explained in Indira Gandhi's reply to Jyotirmoy Bosu, a Member of Parliament belongîng to the CPI(M), in her letter dated 27 November 1972 in which she observed :

> As you know, there is by now a well-settled (i) procedure to examine such memoranda against a chief minister. (ii) He furnishes his comments to me in confidence in order to enable me to determine whether or not there is a need for a commission of inquiry. These comments are not made available even to the complainant... Normally the complainant is not heard before a decision is taken.[13]

The present method of handling complaints of political corruption is nothing if not subjective. There is no objective and uniform procedure as yet for looking into charges of moral lapses on the part of the political executive despite the fact that there has been a legion of allegations of political corruption in India. Thus while the

13. Reproduced in Noorani, A.G. : *Minister's Misconduct*, New Delhi, Vikas: 1973 Appendix VI.

Indira Gandhi government adopted an attitude of total unconcern towards charges of corruption against Haryana's chief minister Bansi Lal it gave an impression of being in over haste in dismissing the Karunanidhi ministry in Tamil Nadu and setting up a probe body against the fallen chief minister and some of his colleagues. The whole procedure for handling charges of political corruption is discretionary, and the central government has been invoking it selectively—to penalise the *persona non grata*, not primarily to uphold political morality.

All the inquiry commissions against political corruption set up so far have consisted of one member only who has invariably been drawn from the higher judiciary of the land. He has been either a sitting or a retired judge. One can easily understand this as the probe work is of a judicial nature and also because there is in India a tradition of complete trust in the integrity of the nation's judiciary. A commission enjoys the freedom to formulate its method of functioning, but the procedure first formulated by Justice S.R. Das in the case of his inquiry against Partap Singh Kairon has become the standard one in the sense it has been consistently observed by all subsequent inquiry bodies. An inquiry commission functions like a judicial body and has generally adopted the procedures normally observed before a court of law. It generally holds its sittings in public and the counsels for both complainant (*i.e.*, memorialists) and the defendent are allowed to appear before it. Memorialists and members of the public are invited to file their affidavits, copies of which are as a rule made available to the defendent who then gives his own comments and files 'counter-affidavits.' If the commission thinks that the filing of any affidavits in reply is necessary, the memorialists have a further opportunity. The commission has also been taking oral evidence. The report of the inquiry commission is made public, which has a deep educative value.

It must not be assumed from the foregoing that determining truth becomes easier as a result of such a balanced procedure. What kind of evidence is ordinarily produced before an inquiry commission and consequently how complex becomes the latter's task can be better understood from the following observation made by one of the commissions. In his report against two ministers in Kerala, A.N. Mulla observed : "

> I would like to make one thing clear at this stage. I will concentrate on the evidence produced before me and the political conflit becomes irrelevant if evidence exists to connect the

defendants with the charges levelled against them. It only makes this difference that the evidence given by the memorialists becomes extremely biased and unless it is satisfactorily corroborated by the entries in the files it would be neither safe nor prudent to place any reliance upon it. Formerly I believed that identification in dacoity cases and the statements of witnesses in communal riot cases was the most unreliable kind of evidence which required the strictest scrutiny before acceptance. Recent experience however compels me to add one more kind of evidence to this list. This is the evidence which is given by witnesses belonging to political groups in cases in which political stakes are involved. An appreciable number of the elected representatives of the people also succumb in such a situation and do not hesitate to make assertions which are far from true. The recent election petition filed against the President of India fully bears out what I have observed above. There was such a clear conflict between the statements of two groups of parliamentarians that one of them was obviously speaking an untruth. It seems that when there is a struggle for power the human clay displays its muddiest surface on top. I will therefore accept the evidence of the memorialists only as far as they are supported by documentary evidence".[14]

The Centre's use of Commissions against states

The first occasion when an inquiry commission was appointed against a member of the country's political executive was in 1964. In that year, Pratap Singh Kairon, the controversial chief minister of Punjab known—and feared during his life time—for the 'Kairon touch' in both politics and administration, was put under a centrally ordered probe. Although the phenomenon of the centre ordering an inquisition against a state level minister was by all means an extra-ordinary constitutional move in a federal polity, its significance or oddity was not much noticed amidst the universal popular relief and joy in having a corrupt and ruthless minister subjected to a judicial investigation. Even Partap Singh Kairon himself, who had practically shelved the constitution while administering his state, had little awareness of any constitutional aberrations the particular measure involved. At any rate, the chief minister belonged to the

14. *Report of the Commissions of Inquiry Consisting of Sri A.N. Mulla In re : Sri M.N. Govindan Nair and Sri T.V. Thomas*, Trivandrum, Government of Kerala, 1971, pp. 7-8.

political party which was in power at the centre also, and a probe practically bore the appearnce of an intra-party affair.

Once the central government discovered this new role for itself it could not remain brief-less, much less under a progressively intolerant political leadership, especially in a federal country which offers opportunities to the centre to treat a state government run by a different party as a thorn in its flesh and worthy only of dismissal. Indira Gandhi, the prime minister from Jannary 1966 to March 1977, had a penchant for toppling governments not of her liking, and the Commission of Inquiry Act assumed a new attraction for her emerging as a stick to beat members of state level political executive with. The second time the inquiry commission was set up was in 1976 when the country was reeling under an authoritarian rule which had rendered democracy, federalism and parliamentarism utterly farcical. In that year the central government under the prime ministership of Indira Gandhi dismissed the D.M.K. ministry under M. Karunanidhi, introduced President's rule in Tamil Nadu, and set up an inquiry commission under the chairmanship of R.S. Sarkaria to look into charges against Karunanidhi and some ex-ministers. The Karunanidhi ministry, to be sure, had earlier protested against any central move to order a probe and told the centre that a state cabinet could not be held accountable to it. Referring to the local opposition demand for a central probe against the D.M.K. Government in Tamil Nadu, the state chief minister said that the constituent states of the Indian Union were "not subordinate to the central government, each state being autonomous within certain defined limits." He argued that every state had a parliamentary form of government and "the cabinet is collectively responsible to the legislative assembly of the state." He continued :

> There is no provision in our constitution which makes the state cabinet accountable to the Union. And as such it would be subversive of entire scheme of the constitution and the system of responsible government if a state cabinet is sought to be subjected to a commission of inquiry constituted by the Union.[15]

It was at one time expected that the Janata Government, which came into power at the Centre in March 1977, would not take recourse to the questionable techniques developed by the Indira

15. *The Times of India*, 15, December 1972.

Gandhi Government. Although the March 1977 parliamentary poll, which swung the Janata Party into power, was a voters' revolution the elements of continuities with the immediate past have been more persistent and powerful. This continuity was manifested most conspicuously in the use of the Commissions of Inquiry Act for the very purposes which made this legislation sensuously appealing to the Congress Party under Indira Gandhi. Bus there appears to be a 'Nehru touch' in the Janata style in as much as centre has mercifully spared the lives of the ministers while putting them on the mat.

The fourth instance—and the first ever under the Janata rule—of use of an inquiry commission was in the case of the Andhra Pradesh chief minister J. Vengal Rao and some of his cabinet colleagues. A section of local opposition legislators (belonging to the party in power at the centre) lodged with the centre a memorandum making allegations of corruption and favourtism against the Congress chief minister and his colleagues. The centre referred the charges to Vengal Rao for his comments and no sooner did his comments reach Delhi than the latter announced a commission under the chairmanship of J.R. Vimadalal to study the charges against the chief minister and some of his colleagues. This was done on 20 May 1977. Surprisingly enough, J. Vengal Rao acted as though completely unconcerned, not even caring to lodge a single protest against the central move ; on the contrary, he is reported to have 'welcomed' the inquiry according to the newspaper reports.

Devaraj Urs, the chief minister of Karnataka, constitutes the fifth instance of the central action against the state level political executive. The story is broadly similar : charges by local opposition legislators, reference to Urs for his comments, and finally the announcement by the central government of an inquiry commission. Devraj Urs, however, would not easily give in, and questioned the propriety of the central move to order a probe against the state level political executive. He observed in his reply to the central home minister on the opposition legislators' charges that the central move to institute an inquiry against a state minister was violative of the federal character of the constitution which has itself distributed administrative and legislative powers between the centre and the state and has put the state government beyoned the centre's orbit of control so far as the states' sphere of functions was concerned. Further, while the constitution provided for the state level ministers' accountability to the state legislature it did not call a state minister to account to the central executive or even to the national Parliament. To attempt to do this was tantamount to robbing the state legislature—and ultimately the people of that state—of the right to have a government of their own free choice. "I reiterate", Devaraj Urs added, "that the central government can have no power to exercise any control over, or to question, the acts of a council of ministers who are responsible to the legislature of the state, and if it is permissible for the central government to inquire into or investigate the acts of the council of ministers in respect of matters within the exclusive jurisdiction of state it would be destructive to the federal structure envisaged by the constitution. . . The cabinet system of government is a basic feature of the Indian constitution. The cabinet functions owes its collective responsibility to the legislature and is subject to the constant vigil of the public—the ultimate judge of a government in a democracy. An inquisitional investigation into the conduct of the council of ministers by an extra constitutional agency, however high, would destroy the basic character of the state and its people the constitutionally guaranteed right of having a government of their choice subject to their control."[16]

These arguments could not in the least convince the Central government, and on 16 May 1977 Morarji Desai, the prime minister, publicly asserted that the centre had a constitutional right to institute a probe into charges of corruption against the state level political executive. Referring to Urs' views mentioned in the preceding paragraph, he gave a rather cryptic reply : "He (Devaraj Urs) is wrong. What they (reference is to the Congress Party to which Urs belongs) did in Tamil Nadu they forget."[17] A retort, however witty, is not necessarily a convincing argument, and a short-sighted action taken in the past particularly during internal emergency (25 June 1975-23 March 1977) when all dissent lay suppressed, can by no means be quoted as a glorious precedent sound for the political system as such.

Meanwhile, the Karnataka chief Minister had himself appointed a commission, under the same Commission of Inquiry Act, to examine the charges which the local opposition had made against him and some other ministers and the terms of reference were made broad enough to cover the allegations that had been made against the previous Veerendra Patil and Nijalingappa ministeries. Whatever be the political motive of Devaraj Urs in the setting up of the probe body he showed by his action that his questioning of the centre's

16. The text of Urs' reply to the charges levelled against him and his colleagues was published in *The Hindu*, 14 May 1977.

17. *Indian Express*, 17 May 1977

power to probe his and his colleagues' actions was not embedded in any desire to ignore or overlook the allegations made by his critics. Hc willingly subjected himself to a probe by a High Court judge to clear the atmosphere 'once for all', as he said.[18] However, as the centre was contemplating a commission against Urs, his himself setting up a body was viewed by the former as being in the nature of pre-empting of the central move. On 23 May 1977 the central government constituted an iuquiry commission headed by A.N. Grover to probe charges of corruption, nepotism and misuse of powers against Devaraj Urs and some other ministers. As a result, two commissions were inquiring against the chief minister and his colleagues. To be sure, the centrally appointed commission was examining additional charges against the Karnataka chief minister and other ministers, but a measure of overlap cannot but be avoided.

Devaraj Urs was not to accept the central announcement of a probe without a further protest. On 31 May 1977 Karnataka filed a suit in the Supreme Court challenging the legality of the appointment of the Grover inquiry body. The arguments advanced by it may be summarised as follows :

1. The constitution has divided the administrative and legislative functions between the centre and the states, and this division impliedly prohibits the centre's control over the state-level executive in the latter's allotted sphere under the constitution. Further, the distribution of function between the two levels of government cannot be changed or supplemented except by an amendment of the constitution.
2. The residuary powers given to parliament under the constitution could not lawfully include the power to enact a law which might vest the control over the state ministers in the central executive, and vice-versa.
3. The constitution makes the state level executive accountable to the assembly and the latter is empowered to withhold confidence in the ministry. This means that the state legislature is clothed with adequate powers to control the state executive, investigate the charges against it and if necessary to censure it and vote it out.
4. The fact of the state executive being subjected to an inquiry before a commission set up by the centre amounts to inter-

18. *The Statesman*, 19 May 1977.

fering with its functioning. This is violative of the federal character of the constitution.

5. The Commission of inquiry Act purports to vest a new power in the central government—the power to institute an inquiry against the ministers of a state. A new power can be conferred only by a constitutional amendment, not by ordinary legislation.

On the other hand, the central government defended its constitutional right to institute a probe against state political executive. To this end it adduced the following arguments :

1. The constitution of India is not truely federal in character. The constitutional distribution of powers, both administrative and legislative, does not confer any immunity on the state and corresponding disability on the centre to order an inquiry against the state level ministers.
2. Parliament is competent to enact the Commissions of Inquiry Act and its power as well as the power of the central government to constitute an investigating commission against the members of the state executive are not subjected to any limitations.
3. An inquiry commission is a fact finding body the object of which is to apprise the centre of certain facts which might emerge from its investigation and which might enable and assist the government to "properly and appropriately exercise its executive powers."
4. The inquiry commission has before it "no prosecution, no charge, no accused." It is, therefore, not correct to say that there is any supervisory or disciplinary jurisdiction over the state.
5. The inquiry commission is a purely recommendatory body and cannot suggest any punishment whatever. It does not, therefore, cause any direct and substantial interference with the executive functions of the state government.

By a majority of six to one, the Supreme Court of India upheld, on 8 November 1977, the central government's constitutional right to appoint such an investigating body. Justice M.H. Beg, the chief justice of India, particularly referred to the patently subservient federal features of the Indian constitution and emphasised that the centre's right in this regard arose, among others, from its dominant unitary spirit. He observed :

> ....Our constitution has, despite whatever federalism may be found in its structure, so strongly unitary features also in it that, when the totality of these provisions is examined, it becomes difficult to assert confidently how much federalism such a constitution contains, whether those parts of its which seem to override the federal elements of our constitution are not more basic or significant than what is described as its federalism.[19]

As the case was heard by a seven-judge constitution bench of the Supreme Court there were separate judgments delivered. The major points made by the Supreme Court may be summarised in what follows. A commission of inquiry is a fact finding body which has no power whatever to pronounce a binding or even definitive judgment. "What is more, the appointment by the central government of a fact-finding commission of inquiry for inquiring into the conduct of sitting state ministers cannot be deemed to vest effective control over the state executive in the central executive."[20] Neither was the concept of collective responsibility of the political executive endangered by a centrally appointed commission of inquiry."[21] "It is difficult to accept that for acts of corruption, nepotism or favourtism which are alleged or proved against an individual minister, the entire council of ministers can be held collectively responsible to the legislature. If an individual minister uses his office as an occasion or pretence for committing acts of corruption, he would be personally answerable for his unlawful acts and no question of collective responsibility of the council of ministers can arise in such a case."[22] Even otherwise, the claim of the state government to have exclusive power to deal with its political executive was not sustainable. "We cannot view allegations of corruption lightly. We think that the interests of the state and of the union are not anti-thetical when there are charges of corruption and misuse of power against those in authority anywhere. To serve the common interests of the whole people, on whose behalf our constitution speaks, the state and the Union cannot stand apart. They must stand together united in purpose and action."[23] Thus, the practice of the Central govern-

19. Taken from the mimeographed copy of the judgment placed in the library of the Supreme Court of India. Judgment in original suit no. 8 of 1977 (state of Karnataka versus Union of India), decided on 8 November 1977, p. 731.
20. Ibid, p. 820
21. Ibid, pp. 812-13
22. Ibid, p. 813
23. Ibid, p. 727

ment appointing a commission of inquiry against the state level political executive "does not bring about any change in the centre-state relationship."[24] Justice P.C. Kailasam, on the other hand, gave a dissenting judgment in which he argued that the centre's action "impinged on the right of the state to function in its limited sphere"[25] and was "beyond the powers conferred on the Union Government under section 3 of the Commissions of Inquiry Act, 1952"[26]. He went on to say that "a commission of inquiry should be strictly in accordance with the constitution and should not affect the centre-state relationship."[27]

Fate of Ministers under probe

There is no uniform practice on whether the ministers, when they are put under a probe, should remain in office or quit. Jawaharlal Nehru vehemently opposed the suggestion that Kairon should resign when the Das Commission was announced. He argued :

> It would be undesirable, I think in the inquiry that is being suggested by me, that the chief minister of Punjab, Sardar Pratap Singh Kairon, should be asked to resign in the course of this inquiry. That would imply that (*prima facie*) there was some truth in the charges made. I do not think we can proceed on that basis . . . There is no reason to believe that his continuance as chief minister during the course will affect the inquiry itself.[28]

And Kairon continued to function as chief minister even while S.R. Das was engaged in his inquiry against him.

Commissions at the state ievel

Many times more have been the commissions appointed by the state governments taken as a whole. In all the states except Kerala it is the executive which has ordered a probe against former minister. In Kerala, on the other hand, the legislative assembly has been from time to time passing resolutions demanding the setting up of inquiry commissions against ministers. Kerala's case has been a rather

24. Ibid, p. 823
25. Ibid, p. 897
26. Ibid, p. 897
27. Ibid, p. 897
28. Jawaharlal Nehru's note to the President recommending the institution of an Inquiry against Pratap Singh Kairon, See Noorani, AG : *op cit*, p. 375

interesting one deserving a special mention. In this state, which has a fairly long-standing political tradition of coalition of parties, not necessarily ideologically very homogeneous, holding the reins of government, the local legislature has been active in passing resolutions demanding inquiries against even the present ministers belonging to constituent parties in the coalition.

Action on the commissions' recommendations

An inquiry commission is a purely recommendatory body and unlike the judicial court's decisions its findings do not have any coercive sanction, whatever, behind them even though its report has its undoubted political importance. While delivering his judgemect in the Devaraj Urs case Supreme Court's Chief Justice M.H. Beg referred to the use as well as limitation of a commission of inquiry in the following :

> A commission of inquiry could not properly be meant, as sometimes suspected, to merely whitewash ministerial or departmental action rather than to explore and discover, if possible, real facts. It is also not meant to serve as a mode of prosecution and much less of persecution. Proceedings before it cannot serve as substitutes for proceedings which should take place before a court of law invested with powers of adjudication as well as of awarding punishments or affording reliefs. Its reports or findings cannot relieve courts which may have to determine for themselves matters dealt with by a commission. Indeed, the legal relevance of evidentiary value of a commission (of inquiry's) report or findings on issues which a court may have to decide for itself is very quesionable. The appointment of a commission of inquiry to investigate a matter which should, in the ordinary course, have gone to a court of law is generally a confession of want of sufficient evidence—as in the case of the appointment of the Warren Commission in the U.S.A. to inquire into facts concerning the murder of the late President Kennedy—to take it to a court combined with an attempt to satisfy the public need and desire to discover what had really gone wrong and how and where, if possible. A commission of inquiry has, therefore, a function of its own to fulfill. It has an orbit or action of its own within which it can move so as not to conflict with or impede other forms of action or modes of redress...[29]

29. Justice M.H. Beg's judgment in suit number 8 (State of Karnataka Versus Union of India), pp. 748-49

If an inquiry body has found someone guilty of corruption there are three options open to the government. More often than not, the government has as a deliberate policy shelved it and has taken no action whatever. This was the fate met by inquiries against Bakshi Ghulam Mohammed (Jammu-Kashmir), K.B. Sahay (Bihar), Mahamaya Prasad Sinha (Bihar), Biju Patnaik (Orissa,) Harekrishna Mehtab (Orissa) etc. Sometimes the government has taken a modicum of action against the political figure involved by inducing him to resign 'voluntarily' from his office, and the matter is allowed to rest there with no further action contemplated against him. This was what happened to Pratap Singh Kairon. The government may also take the case to the law court and seek the individual's punishment. This is the course which has been opted for in the case of Karunanidhi ; on receipt of Sarkaria commission's interim reports the central government launched legal action against Tamil Nadu's former chief minister.

Though political corruption in India has been fairly widespread there was a conspicuous absence of a regular and systematised arranagement of investigating charges in this field. The existing practice is hundred percent discretionary, and has not been without inevitable political colourings. It requires the local political system to gear up and intensify an agitation in favour of a particular probe before it can be ordered ; and it can be ordered only if the central government is sympathetic towards the demand. The Commissions of Inquiry Act has no momentum of its own. Even otherwise, 'grey areas' of public life do not lend themselves to this kind of a political manipulation. Also, under such an arrangement it is not entirely uncommon for the centre even to prompt with discreet silence the local dissident legislators to ask for investigation against the political executive, especially when that particular state government and the central government are under the control of different political parties. Either of such actions keeps alive a climate of political uneasiness and unrest in the country. To put differently, an inquiry commission against political corruption has very often been treated as a weapon to harass political opposition. Those who get on the wrong side of the power structure at the centre are often made to face the 'squad'.

A substantially large number of charges against ministers have been found be the various inquiry commissions to be true; and thus the probe bodies have indeed served public interest by exposing corruption at high places even though punishment has not followed in all the cases. Also, unfailingly the commissions have repeatedly referred to the growing linkages between ministers and civil servants (and also private industry) in acts of wrong-doing, thereby tending to make corruption a more organised affair. Quid pro quo-ism is firmly ingrained in India's emerging political culture.

The largest number of commissions against political corruption have been launched by the state governments. The usual immediate background for the inquisitorial phenomenon is a change in the political complexion of the ruling party in the state : a state government run by a party or coalition different from its preceding one has often ordered a probe against the members of the preceding government. Among the state governments Kerala has appointed the largest number of commissions of inquiry against alleged ministerial misconduct, but one should not be in a haste to infer that Kerala ministers alone are any worse than the ministers in those states where no such probe bodies have been set up. Otherwise, the conclusion would be that all cases of political corruption in India are getting systematically unearthed and the politicians probed by inquiry bodies are the only ones who have been suspected of being wanting in integrity. For from this. Appointment of a probe body is a decision based on political considerations. Dismaying though it may sound, the device of an inquiry commission against political personages have been very often employed with deleterious selectivity in India. When the investigating net is thrown wide open it may in all likelihood come to light that corruption is today a nearly integral part of the dynamics of politics and public administration in India.

It is inevitable in the process that inquiry commissions may some times be used, or at least be suspected of being used, for political baiting. This was the fear expressed by one of the commissions of inquiry, and its chairman even regarded its own commission's appointment as being politically motivated. Justice A.N. Mulla, the chairman of the commission of inquiry appointed by Kerala to examine allegations against M.N. Govindan Nair and T.V. Thomas, was constrained to remark that "there is an atmosphere of unreality about the institution of this inquiry commission. I feel that this commission of inquiry is only an added front for a political fight and not a tribunal set up for administrative reasons."[30] He cautioned the government against any easy recourse to this

30. *Report of the Commission of Inquiry consisting of Sri A.N. Mulla in re : Sri M. N. Govindan Nair and Sri T.V. Thomas*, Trivandrum, Government of Kerala, 1971. p.7. ('In re:, an expression used in legal cases, means 'in the matter of'),

mechanism. "I suggest", he observed, "that such inquiries should not be lightly started for this defeats the very purpose of these inquiries. If this continues no one will take the reports of these commissions seriously and they will be treated just as a part of the political fight...I think a commission of inquiry should be constituted only for administrative reasons and that too when there are good grounds to believe that a major deviation from the path of probity is noticeable in the conduct of minister and not on some minor lapses which can safely be dealt with in some other manner."[31]

Impact on Federalism

There is a more serious criticism of the employment of this device for fighting corruption. The centre's use of inquiry commissions against the state level political executive does not appear to be in complete harmony with the spirit of the constitution despite the Supreme Court of India's recent endorsement of such a right. Federalism and parlimentarism are the two inalienable features of the constitution, and the centrally directed probes are at odds with them. The central government in India, itself a creation of a federal constitution, must respect the demarcation of functions between the two levels of government and an attempt to call to books the state level political executive involves a dangerous departure from the accepted federal practices. It is argued on behalf of the centre that it can appoint a commission of inquiry to look into matters covered by list II or list III. But nowhere in either of these lists does explicitly figure an item like misdeeds of the political executive at the state level. Nor does the Commission of Inquiry Act, 1952 confer any explicit power upon the centre to inquire into the conduct of the ministers of a state. The political executive in India's parliamentary system of government owes direct responsibility to the legislature, and the latter alone is competent to take it to task, for which it stands adequately equipped. This accountability is direct, continuous and indivisible and cannot be made subordinate to any externally induced loyalty.

Nor is any real gain achieved by imposing on the parliamentary system of government the structure and the spirit of unitarism. The present arrangement governing the invocation of an inquiry against political corruption is neither automatic nor assured nor equitable. Under the present practice it depends upon the centre to decide when a probe is to be ordered, what its terms of reference are to be,

31, Ibid, p. 154.

who are to be the persons against whom it is to be directed, etc. Like any other govrenment, the central government is a party one, and cannot escape but be guided by its own political calculus in the appointment of such probe bodies or for that matter, in the follow-up of the reports. At any rate, its actions will always be suspected. What has happened is that the central government has, in this respect, made political morality tenuous in its apparent concern for political "integrity" at one (that is, state) level of the government only.

The central government at present finds itself safe and secure in its use of inquiry commissions as highest judiciary of the land has upheld its right of a probe against the state-level political executive. But this does not genuinely solve the problem in a long range respective. Federalism, be it noted, is not *all* constitution only, much less *all* law only : it has powerful extra-constitutional and extra-legal dimensions which supply vitality to it and make it a functioning concept. 'Political' is the short-hand for these extra-dimensions. Federalism, in the ultimate analysis. is a political device, and its fundamental problems demand political solutions, not judicial verdicts only, for nursing by the polity alone can confer complete legitimacy. The political system of the country, therefore, must consciously seek to look at the constitution in this perspective also. Even if the centre is legally correct in setting up an inquiry commission against state level ministers this right will prove to be more effective when it is held in abeyance. The centre ordering probes against the state executive will always continue to be felt as a mote in the states' eyes, and will ever disturb the central-state harmony.

This is not to overlook, much less condone, breaches of integrity in the politicial life of the country. But lack of probity is not necessarily a feature of the state level political executive only. Recruitment to the political cadres of both the central and the state governments takes place from the same source and it would be manifestly unfair and incorrect to ascribe political foibles to the state level only. No level of government can be completely and eternally immune to corruption and arrogance of power. What is necessary, therefore, is the creation of a standing machinery which can swing itself into action when moral lapses on the part of the political executive of either level are monitored. An ombudsman-like institution needs to be set up in India.

Equally important—and more so in the long run—is the need for fostering and maintaining a continually differentiating, and autonomous social system at the state level—and even below it—to oversee the functioning of the various branches of the government and call for action when deviations are noticed. Decentralisation can be effective and fruit bearing only if a favourable climate at the local level has been created in its favour. There must be suitable infra-structure to over-see that what is decentralised gets put into action efficiently and honestly. In other words, there must be at the local level, in this case the state level, well differentiated, diversified autonomous sectors of activities to keep watch on the behaviour of people in political authority and call for action when wrongs are committed. Our cultivated habit of not rising up, speaking the truth and demanding action in time when transgressions are made is inimical to a sound practice of decentralisation.

One may also argue that motivations of those who conceive and enact a piece of legislation and those who are to apply it do not happen to be identical. On the contrary, the original intentions underlying a legislative measure are almost as a rule obscured. and displaced by new meanings discovered in old provisions. This is much more so in the case of the articles of the constitution and the laws which are of a general import. Not only are new interpretations given and new justifications offered, but the second generation meanings, too, do not hold good for very long, for these are overtaken by still newer ones. And the cycle continues. This constitutes on less than invisible legislation-making by the executive of the day. Should not, then, the legislature stop enacting laws valid for eternity, as it were ? It may perhaps be considered whether it will not be more prudent to pass laws which would hold good for a stipulated period only and would lapse after the expiry date unless re-enacted.

9

POLITICAL CORRUPTION

THERE IS hardly any issue which is so much discussed and arouses so much concern and indignation in India—even if at the level of rhetoric—as that of corruption. Corruption in this country is widespread and, what is more, has been on the increase over the years. Many have even come to believe that it has almost become a way of life in India.

There was no time in the history of India when corruption could be said not to have existed in its public life including administration. This was confirmed by Kautilya in his celebrated *Arthashastra*. It existed under the British Raj, too, but generally speaking only in certain sectors of administration such as lower levels of the police, the judiciary, excise and so on and in small doses.

CONSEQUENCE

Never was it viewed as a serious problem, though it increased perceptibly in the course of the Second World War, characterized as it was by Governmental control and rationing of scarce articles of common use. Corruption cannot be regarded as the legacy of the Raj. It is a consequence, though unintended, of the type of political processes and the pattern of development India has conciously chosen.

Indian political system has its anchorage in elections the latter constituting, so to say, its power-house. An election is the functional equivalent, or counterpart, of a public service commission, and a politically ambitious citizen has to graduate into politics through it and what is more the process has to be repeated at regular intervals. But elections are proving to be very expensive and are becoming increasingly so over the years, in contemptuous disregard of the ceiling on expenditure prescribed by the Election Commission of India. A constituency in India is large and sprawling and touring by the candidate, his supporters and campaigners would cost a lot. He must mobilise a fleet of vehicles to reach voters in different parts of the campaign area. He has necessarily to provide for publicity material and arrange for its timely distribution. For successful campaigning he thus needs monetary resources and manpower, most of his workers being mercenaries. An average politician, not unnaturally, comes from an ordinary economic background, and has to depend on others for the financing of his election. It is precisely this which has given birth to the linkage politics and the linkage politician. He seeks links with those who command money power.

When the politician was casting his eyes broad and wide in search of financial wherewithal, the financier was also emerging on the scene and what is more looking for him. This financier was the business man—a generic expression including the industrialist, contractor and the like. This phenomenon owed itself to the operational model of development India has opted for itself. Development through planning within the framework of mixed economy, India's choice, made state the prime mover in the field conferring unlimited discretion and patronage into the hands of ministers. Even an ordinary politician commanded influence in the decision-making processes, for the minister, derives none too insignificant measure of his support from the politicians.

The inter-face between politics and business began to develop with the First Five Year Plan (1951-56) itself, the much talked about Mudgal case being the pointer to the slowly unfolding relationship. But it became close with the Second Five Year Plan (1956-61), which was heavily industry-oriented and envisaged, moreover, huge public expenditure. As a result, the Government discovered itself in a rather novel role. It had lot to give, and to control, and the politician, already looking round gree ily, extracted a price for his patronage. The early sixties was a period in India thick with rumours about corruption at the highest political level and these rumours were also generally confirmed by the S.R. Das Commission of Inquiry against Punjab's controversial Chief Minister, Pratap Singh Kairon (1964) and the K. Santhanam Committee on Prevention of Corruption (1964). The Committee on Prevention of Corruption observed :

> The sudden extension of the economic activities of the Government with a large armoury of regulations, controls, licenses and permits provided new and large opportunities. The quest for political power at different levels made successful achievement of the objective more important than the means adopted. Complaints against the highly placed in public life were not dealt with if public confidence had to be maintained. Weakness in this respect

created cynicism and the growth of the belief that while Governments were against corruption they were not against corrupt individuals, if such individuals had the requisite amount of power, influence and protection.[1]

The Santhanam Committee on Prevention of Corruption made as many as 137 recommendations including that for the immediate establishment of the Central Vigilance Commission. The latter body has been set up and many other recommendations too have been carried out but corruption far from getting checked became even more widespread touching new heights and reaching new intensities. There have been no less than nineteen commissions of inquiry set up by the central and state governments since 1947 to examine, among others, charges of corruption against political leaders and all of them have generally confirmed in varying ways the veracity of such charges. It should also be noted that what these commission have pointed out is but the tip of the ice-berg and does not disclose its true dimensions. Such investigative bodies are set selectively generally on political motivations and thus uncover only a very small part of what is the true state of affairs.

The emerging corruption in India bears certain attributes worth public attention. It is basically politico-administrative in nature in the sense that it is not an isolated phenomenon but rather engulfs the the political as well as administrative levels in government. It has thus deeper roots, is well organised and systematic. Secondly, it originates at the top political and administrative levels, which sharply distinguishes it from the corruption of the traditional variety, confined as it generally was to only lower level public functionaries in certain areas of administration. It is because of the involvement of the top levels that its eradication, today, becomes very difficult. Thirdly, the emergent corruption is not petty, running as it does into which may be considered to be astronomical figures. Fourthly, over the years corruption has acquired immense sophistication and has developed new forms and shapes. It is not necessarily in the shape of money ; it may acquire a form corresponding to the weakness of the person who had to do the particular work. The business man, the politician and the civil servant have generally formed an alliance so to say and the last mentioned two have subordinated themselves to the will of the first. Indeed, many politicians, taking advantage of their powers

1. *Report of the Committee on Prevention of Corruption, New Delhi,* Ministry of Home Affairs, Government of India, 1964, pp. 7-8.

and position, have themselves set up their business, especially in areas where fast buck is assured such as entertainment industry, land and building, government contracting, etc. Sixthly, the earlier view that corruption is a peculiar characteristic of the Congress rule alone does not appear to be very correct. It became nearly characteristic of the Janata Party which remained in power from 1977 to 1979.

Nor is corruption a purely governmental phenomenon. The trade union hierarchy is only scarcely less vulnerable, its members not hesitating to demand bribes for getting done the work of the individual employees and even of the employers. This is perhaps equally true of voluntary organisations. The purchase officer in a private organisation is as corrupt as the administrative head in an academic organisation. Corruption, in short, has become horizontal and modern India seems to be floating on it. That the formally professed policies and plans get distorted and a parallel government verily emerges and holds sway over the people inevitably follows. It is the writ of this parallel government which runs in not a few sectors and areas of life.

Hard decisions are needed to curb, if not eliminate, corruption, India's foremost problem. First and foremost, the political culture of India must change if corruption is to be dealt with very firmly. Elections must be made cheap, at any rate substantially less expensive than what they presently are. Indeed, electoral reform is essential if the society desires a politician with a different orientation to emerge. Tied with electoral reform is the need for reform in the management of the political parties. Political parties of the land must be brought under a measure of public discipline. They must be obliged to maintain their accounts which must be audited and made public. Thirdly, the society should make politics less glamorous and take some gloss off it. The elections are present at fought at an extraordinarily high pitch precisely because the stakes are too high : the winner at once gets shot into a charmed world of almost unlimited facilities and perks, of unmatched power and pelf. An elected politician enjoys a vast range of facilities and patronage, both visible and invisible, and a wrong spirited one even more. No other career in India offers such an intensive package of power and perquisites, which naturally has an effect of setting its member apart from the rest of the society. Fourthly, it would do good to realize that laws of the market may be more fair than the discretionary powers of the minister and the style cultivated by Abdul Rehman Antulay, the former chief minister of Maharashtra, should be an eye-opener to the society. Increasingly, the governmental power of regulation and control, of granting permits and licences is being used for blatantly partisan purposes, and a clean public life would demand that the state should restrict the area of permits and licences. Fifthly, corruption flows in no uncertain way from a situation of shortages and scarcities ; and the national effort ought to be directed to raise productivity. The coal industry and the electricity boards, which are guilty of under-production, are, for instance, encouraging corruption by their slack habits alone and should re-orient their ways. Besides, there is no harm if the Government itself, where feasible, sells certain categories of goods and services at a premium. A citizen already pays some extra at present to get his thing done but while now the money is to fructify in the private pocket it will be enabled to flow into the public treasury under this arrangement. Sixthly, laws of the land, especially taxation laws must be enforced with uniform strictness so that the deviants may get booked and the society is rescued from the shame of having a parallel economy, thriving on black money. It is not insignificant that 'black money' is estimated to have increased from Rupees 400 crores in 1959 to Rs. 15,000 Rs. 25,000 crores in the eighties, and the rise has been dramatic particularly from 1973 onwards. Tax morality must be restored, and tax administration must be made effective.

Also, the inflationary trend in the economy must be checked, for integrity finds itself under considerable strains in a situation of rising price level. Seventhly, appropriate reforms in the machinery of government and its procedures of work must be urgently carried out, for at present the administrative procedures are so cumbersome and complicated that a citizen, unable to comprehend and follow them, sees no way out except to bribe the officials to get his even lawful work done. Attempts at containment of corruption cannot be very rewarding unless they are reinforced by reform in the country's public administration. In the eighth place, an organised effort should be made to expose the black sheep in the society and their deeds ; and the society must create investigative squads or watch-dog organisations for this purpose. The should uphold morality and chastise defaulters in all walks of life—politics, bureaucracy, medicine, teaching, etc.

The press in India can really play a vital role in this regard. Besides, the country must set up a permanent machinery to check corruption including the political one. The Parliament should lose no time in setting up the institutions of Lokpal and Lokayukta endowing them with wide powers and bringing the political executive also under its ambit. The recommendation for

Lokpal was first made in 1967, and the Government had accepted it too. It is a pity that the necessary legislation has not yet been enacted. Twice in the last twelve years the bill to set up the functionary was introduced in the parliament but was not carried through, which is perhaps suggestive of a lukewarm parliamentary attitude towards the proposed institution. Finally and very importantly, ethical values must be resuscitated and disseminated in the society, particularly among the members of the ruling ellte. Historically, men have desisted from doing many unjust, immoral things under the fear of God but God has been displaced by Mammon under the emergent values and the void thus created is shaping an amoral man, whose goal is success in total disregard of the means.

These suggestions constitute an integrated whole, and package deal so to say and must be acted upon simultaneously. The need for simultaneous action on a broader front is particularly emphasized in the context of a popular belief that the problem of corruption would be solved once the institution of Lokpal is set up. The proposed Lokpal can be effective in a society in which corruption prevails in restricted measures and specific areas only. Corruption is too widespread in India for the Lokpal, and the latter functionary needs reinforcements and support structures. But all this is possible only when there is firm political and bureaucratic will to view corruption as a malignant growth and to rid the society of it.

10

CENTRE-STATE RELATIONS

FEDERALISM IS a political mechanism to manage within a single framework multiple territorial personalities which, in its absence, would have either chalked out their individual destinies and thus fallen apart or got choked out of their separate existence and thus indistinguishably assimilated in a monolithic system. Recognition of a dual polity is thus the quintescence of federalism and yet a complete harmony between them is humanly impossible to achieve, notwithstanding a written constitution. All federal systems encounter problems and imbalances in the area of inter-governmental relations, no matter how detailed and elaborate is the distribution of functions and resources between the two levels. This is essentially because the process of adjustment is a dynamic one. The problem is all the more acute in the case of India for two very important reasons. The framers of the Indian Constitution,[1] were not as free as, say, the framers of the American Constitution who had only the declaration of a few principles to guide them. In contrast, the Constituent Assembly of India functioned closely within the mental framework of the Government of India Act, 1935 with its strong unitary bias. Indeed, the whole body of administrative folklore of India was distinctly unitary and thus favourable to the central government. This culture was powerfully reinforced by the partition-borne psychology of the time. Partition of India accompanied by riots in various parts of the country, followed by Pakistani aggression in Jammu-Kashmir, provided the immediate environment for constitution-making in India. The Constitution of India is a true child of its times.

CONSTITUTIONAL FRAMEWORK

The centre-state relations in India have always contained seeds of conflict, and this partly flows from the arrangements made in the

1. For a more detailed discussion of the subject, see S.R. Maheshwari : *State Governments in India*, New Delhi, Macmillan, 1979, especially chapter on 'Centre-State Relations', pp. 220-244.

constitution itself. The Constitution of India made the states deeply subordinate to, and dependent on the centre in various ways, which was a departure from the federal principle originally put forward under the Cabinet Mission Plan of 16 May 1946. The legislative, administrative and financial arrangements devised in the supreme document unmistakably betray the centrist culture. Indeed, the central government, which emerges from the constitutional postulates, is, in addition, the government of the governments in India. The manner of creation of all-India services, of transfer of functions from state list to union list, etc., are among the instances of the Constitution's solicitation for the centre. On the top of it, it empowers the centre to dismiss a state-level ministry and introduce President's rule. Besides, the constitution confers major programmatic responsibilities on the states, and as such both the components of development and regulatory administration are directly in the state's field of action. But the resource-yielding powers are mostly given to the centre, thereby making the states generally dependent on the centre for financial support. This was part of the larger scheme of keeping the states under the centre's discipline and even control. The imbalance between functions and resources has been persistently aggravated by the operational realities of the polity.

The dependence syndrome has become stronger with the adoption of planning in India since 1950 and the single party dominance system in the country. Planning is a centralising process for it consciously works for the uniformity of policy over the entire field of public administration both at the centre and in the states. The Constitution of India has set up a horizontal federation whereas the Planning Commission has converted it into a vertical one : the central and state departments on the same portfolios have come to form, so to say, a unit for purposes of planning, programming and expenditure. Centralisation received powerful reinforcement from the single party dominance system of the land. The fact of the Congress Party being in power at both the levels of government nearly made the centre-state relations correspond to those between the Pradesh Congress Committees and the 'High Command'. When the same party is in power at the centre and in the states, the problems between them begin to be examined along the party network, and to that extent the constitution remains in disuse. Under the single party dominance system, the centre's relationship with a particular state came to depend on the political stature of its leadership and the equation it had with the central leaders. But with men like Pandit Jawaharlal Nehru, Sardar Vallabhbhai Patel, Abdul Kalam Azad,

Govind Ballabh Pant, etc., being at the centre, the state level political leadership easily acquiesced in the central behests, thus buildlng up traditions favourable to the centre even though it is also true that the tilt towards the centre was somewhat countered by the central leaders' own dependence on the local leaders for political and party support.

Nor should one forget that the resource base of the states, never very satisfactory, has even suffered abridgement by certain actions of the centre like merging of income-tax paid by companies with corporate tax and pre-empting to itself a large percentage of the draft on private savings and resources. Though the state governments are presently getting nearly 53 per cent of the total tax revenues as a result of the recommennations of the Seventh Finance Commission, their resources are actually inadequate in terms af their developmental needs. This shortage of funds is not to provide relief to the tax-payer. Not in the least. The larger share of revenues remains to roost with the centre, which may enable it to indulge in extravagance. There are other anomalies too. A state government is entitled to overdrafts up fo two per cent of its annual expenditure at 13 per cent interest. But for the Central Government, there is no such limit, and the rate of interest is also 6.5 per cent. This plainly is a discriminatory arrangement with no apparent justification.

Planning Commission and Finance Commission

Broadly-speaking, the transfer of resources from the centre to the states many materialise along three channels. The first is the Finance Commission which lays down the formula for sharing of tax revenues, the second is the Planning Commission which allocates outlay for various sectors under Article 282 of the Constitution, and the third is classified as 'other transfers by the Government of India.' Both the Finance Commission and the Planning Commission deserve a second look today. As is common knowledge, the Finance Commission is a constitutional body, but the Planning Commission has been set up merely under an executive resolution. Yet the latter has emerged as a more powerful body restricting, in practice, the scope and functions of the Finance Commission. What has happened in practice is that the Finance Commission finds itself reduced to the level of a body which is merely to determine the revenue gap of each state and provide for its filling up through a scheme a devolution—by grants-in-aid and sharing of taxes and duties. This is contrary to the intention of the constitution-makers, for, as visualised by them, the Finance Commission was to be the most active and powerful body in regulating central-state financial relations in India.[2] Besides, the divisible pool of taxes, which falls within the jurisdiction of the Finance Commission, must be considerably enlarged, especially in view of the centre's practice of levying non-divisible surcharges on corporate taxes. The states should be given a larger share than what they are getting at present. The corporate tax and the surcharge on income-tax must be included in the divisible pool. Besides, they presently encounter many other handicaps also. Those not in the good books of the centre may find it very difficult to secure adequate resources which are presently commanded by nationalised banks, Life Insurance Corporation, and other public financing institutions. The location of industries in a state is also determined by the industrial policies and licensing procedures of the central government. It may thus be seen that the financial and economic position of the state goverments is inevitably affected by the deeds and decisions of the centre.

What is more, the Finance Commission at present is deeply one-sided in its approach. While it can examine the financial needs of the states, it lacks authority to look into the financial requirements of the centre and to allocate funds to it accordingly. In other words, the centre obliges the states to accept a kind of discipline from which it itself stands completely released ! The anomaly must be removed. This points to the need for an Expenditure Commission to subject the centre also to a wide ranging scrutiny. Nor should one forget that the central government has hardly set a good example before the states in the matter of husbanding resources. In 1973-74, the total central revenue receipts were Rs. 5072 crores while the revenue expenditure was Rs. 4,835 yielding a surplus of Rs. 237 crores. But in 1982-83 the expenditure was Rs. 18,227 crores against a revenue receipt of only Rs. 17,130 crore. The central government apparently accepts little fiscal discipline over itself. Both its control over the government mint and easy access to international financing institutions have made it less inclined to practise financial austerity of a type which is normally expected of it.

Governor

The Governor's[3] office is extra-ordinarily important in the regulation of relationship between the centre and the states, and yet it has

2. See the note by the Chairman of the Fourth Finance Commission. *Report of the Fourth Finance Commission*, Delhi: Government of India, 1966, pp. 80-90.
3. Also see S.R. Maheshwari : *State Governments in India*, *op. cit.*, pp. 33-45.

suffered distortions since the in auguration of the constitution. This functionary is no longer viewed as being completely impartial and non-partisan in the performance of his responsibilities. Indeed, he is increasingly showing signs of becoming the proverbial thorn in the political flesh of the opposition-ruled state. It is in the interest of over-all political harmony that his powers and position be codified to put his behaviour above controversy. The practice of 'transfer' of governors, first introduced in 1966, does not add to the prestige of the constitutional office nor do their frequent visits to Delhi for 'consultations' look very dignified. The governor does not today enjoy even a semblance of initiative in the introduction of President's rule in a state : the centre takes the decision, and he is made to undergo the ritual of forwarding his report. Ne set criteria have been formulated in respect of who is to be invited to be the chief minister and when is the legislature to be dissolved. In the non-Congress States the governor exercises, since 1984, his discretion in the appointment of the vice-chancellor of a university but one is not sure if the practice would be allowed to extend to the Congress-ruled states too.

Other Imbalances

Besides problems of financial nature, some other imbalances have also crept into the system for want of care. To cite an example, the constitution provides for freedom of expression, which means freedom to write, to speak, to inform and yet the most powerful mass media in India is a state monopoly ; and citizens are prohibited from setting up private radio and television stations. What is more, the state government themselves stand debarred from having their independent arrangements in this field. Many provisions of the Government of India Act, 1935 were transplanted in the constitution in an apparently thoughtless way, and it is time such incongruities are identified and corrected.

The Constitution of India confers two sets of roles on the central government. The centre is itself a level of government, enjoying defined powers and functions—just as states do. Over and above, the central government is also the government of the governments in India, and in this capacity it carries out a large number of functions. Article 356, providing for President's rule in the states, is a policing and disciplining constitutional provision which amply testifies to the centre being the government of the governments in India. Though these are two different categories of roles, the constitution does not provide for distinct and separate mechanisms for carrying them out. It is but proper for a government formed on party lines to conduct the affairs in the first category according to its own party philosophy, but the role of the government of the governments in India demands a more broad-based machinery actuated by supra-party interests. It is the absence of such a mechanism which is bedeviling the centre-state relations in India.

Profiles of State Government

One must not necessarily conclude from the foregoing that the state governments are absolutely clean and honest in their dealings and deeds while the centre alone is at fault. They themeselves have been reproducing the centre's image when interaction with the lowest level government is involved. Many of the states have not taken planning very seriously : and do not plan within their known resources or have not incorporated the needs of overall integrated development of the entire state. Many of the states have not yet constituted statutory planning bodies. But they go on demanding from the centre massive irrigation and power projects while those already in hand languish in their states uncompleted entailing enormous cost escalations. Many of them have been negligent in managing their affairs prudently. For instance, the aggregate losses incurred by the State Road Transport Corporations were Rs. 62.35 crores in 1979-80 and are likely to touch the figure of Rs. 1340 crores during 1980-85. Electricity was a paying item when it was in private sector, but after nationalisation nearly all electricity boards are incurring huge losses and, what is more, keeping the citizens starved of electricity.

The states' own mismanagement of their resources may produce an inclination in them to search for scapegoats. There is thus a fear of the centre-state relations getting turned into an anti-centre tirade, partly to cover up the inadequacies and failures of the individual state itself. Soberly speaking, there is no basic incompatibility between a strong centre and strong states, and the governing principals in cooperative federalism should be : who collects the funds is not very relevant, for funds flow from the people ; what is important is that the levels of government needing them the most must not remain deprived of them. Nor should one forget that the taxes come from the citizens and only such load of these should be placed on them as is absolutely unavoidable. At the same time, utmost efficiency and economy must be practised by all levels of government in managing their affairs, and the electricity board culture must be condemned. Administrative reform, one may venture to suggest, must be regarded as an integral part of the larger process of sharing of functions and resources within the governmental system.

A step-motherly treatment of local government at the hands of the state governments has been referred to, but this aspect needs elaboration. Federalism is discovered to be increasingly inadequate in its traditional coverage, and this can be made up by incorporating local government as an integral level of a federal system. Local government, today, is a vital level of the government system for it meets the basic day-to-day needs of the citizens, and yet it is in a state of neglect in most states. It must be accorded constitutional base with its autonomous tax-zone and a respectable sharing of federal revenues. The students of political science and public administration must re-tune themselves, and begin also to talk of local government when discussing federalism. Federalism must be made a three-tier concept.

HISTORY OF REFORM OF CENTRE-STATE RELATIONS

The problems of Indian federalism have been discussed by three committees which have been set up since the inauguration of the constitution. The period of 1950-66 was characterised by the dominance of the Congress Party as the ruling party in the centre and in most states, and as such any major questions of centre-state relations did not arise, atleast in the open. The fourth general election (1967) changed for the first time the political complexion of the country as the Congress was defeated in several states in India. As a result, other parties came into power, and problems of centre-state relationship became acute, for the first time. The states mounted a campaign for a restructuring of relationship in a bid to have a higher measure of autonomy. Just before the election, the Central Government had appointed an Administrative Reforms Commission (ARC) whose terms of reference included examination of centre-state relations also. The ARC constituted a Study Team under M.C. Setalvad to carry out a comprehensive examination of this problem. The Study Team submitted its Report in 1968. Making it as the basis, the ARC finalised its own report on the subject in 1969. The central action in setting up a commission to examine inter-governmental relations did not completely satisfy the states. At any rate, Tamil Nadu constituted, in 1969, a Centre-State Relations Inquiry Committee under P.V. Rajamanmar to inquire into this field and make recommendations for improving the relations. This committee submitted its report in 1971. The period 1966-70 was one of extreme political fluidity in the country making centre-station relations a subject of keen controversy. The controversy was continuously fanned by the manner of use of Article 356 providing for President's rule in the states. In a short period of four years 1967-71, there occurred eleven instances of President's rule in the states. The seventies saw the reverse swing of the pendulum, and the Congress again became nearly the dominant party in the land. Questions of centre-state relations thus ceased to be matters of public controversy and consequently got relegated to the background. The weakening of the hold of the Congress Party and the coming into power of other parties in a number of states, since 1982, have again revived this question. Pressed hard, the Central Government announced, in August 1983, constitution of a commission under the chairmanship of Justice R.S. Sarkaria to go into centre-state relations and recommend appropriate changes within the present constitutional framework. The commission is expected to submit its report by the middle of 1985.

The Setalvad Study Team had recommended constitution of an Inter-State Council composed of the prime minister and other central ministers holding key portfolios, chief ministers and others, invited or co-opted. It suggested measures to rationalise the relationship between the Finance Commission and the Planning Commission. Besides, it recommended that the office of governor be filled by a person having ability, objectivity and independence and the incumbent must regard himself as a creation of the constitution, and not as an official of the central government. The Administrative Reforms Commission noticed that the central government had even moved into the field earmarked for the states under the constitution and asked it to withdraw from it. It recommended the setting up of an inter-state council but made a novel suggestion about its composition. Instead of giving seats in this body to all the the chief ministers, it wanted to have five representatives—one each from the five zonal councils. Moreover, the ARC highlighted the need for formulation of guidelines to govern the exercise of discretionary powers by the governor. This would ensure uniformity of action and eliminate all suspicions of partisanship or arbitrariness on the part of this functionary. It also recommended that the question whether a chief minister enjoys majority support or not should be tested on the floor of the legislature and for this he should summon the the assembly whenever a doubt arises. It also opined that when a ministery suffers a defeat in the legislative assembly on a major policy issue and if the outgoing chief minister advises the governor to dissolve the assembly with a view to obtaining the verdict of the electorate, the Governor should normally accept the advice.

The Rajamannar Centre-State Relations Inquiry Committee recommended the setting up of an Inter-State Council but its compotion was on lines substantially different from those laid by the ARC. It recommended that the Council should comprise all the chief ministers, headed by the prime minister. It observed :

> No other Minister of the Union Cabinet should be a member of the Council. The Governor should be appointed in consultation with the State government and he should be ineligible for second term of office as Governor or any other office under the Government. He should have a fixed tenure and is not to be removed except for proved misbehaviour or incapacity after inquiry by the Supreme Court. These provisions are calculated to make him independent of the central political leadership in the discharge of his responsibilities. Further, the jurisdiction of Article 356 of the Constitution should be restricted, and the only contingency which may justify the imposition of President's rule under Article 356 is the complete breakdown of law and order in a state, when the State Government itself is unable or unwilling to maintain the safety and security of the people and property in the state.[4]

The Committee's other recommendations include transfer of some functions from the concurrent to the state list and re-definition of some items in the union list. It moreover, wanted residuary power of legislation and taxation to vest in the state legislature.

The 282-page Rajamannar Report came out in 1971 but it proved to be still-born, because action on it lay in the hands of the centre. But the Central Government has been uniform in its treatment of all reports : none has gained any acceptance, even in part. The recommendations of its own committees have fared no better.

Concluding observation

The dynamics of both democracy and development has significantly changed the framework in which the states now find themselves operating, thus signifying a need for a wide-ranging re-examination of centre-state relations so that they are enabled to have adequate

4. *Report of the Centre-State Relations Inquiry Committee*, Madras, Government of Tamil Nadu, 1971, p. 24,

powers as well as resources to meet their growing needs. This is possible without weakening the centre.

Federalism, one may note, is created by a constitution, but what sustains it is politics itself. On closer analysis, it will be discovered that the problem of Indian federalism is an exercise in politics. The nuances of this relationship are all political and are not immediately derived from the constitution. The problem of centre-state relationship is basically one of relationship between the political leadership at the central and state levels, which calls for greater sensitivity to the need for development of sound political processes and conventions in the land.

11

TENSION-AREAS IN INDIAN POLITICS

INDIAN POLITICS is entering a new period of turbulence and turmoil. Part of the ensuing turbulence is a direct consequence of the success of the democratic and developmental processes underway since Independence but another part flows from the leadership's ineptitude in management of public affairs. Old structures are crumbling, and the nation must set out to evolve a new framework of political development. The present chapter seeks to identify the crucial tension-areas in the country's politics and to suggest an agenda for action also.

TENSION AREAS

The Congress Party,[1] which spearheaded the national mevement for Independence, has remained continuously in power at the centre (except for a brief period of two and a half years) and in most states since 1947, which provided a uniquely stable framework for policy-making and administration in the country, For the first time, the Congress was defeated in the elections held in 1977, but it returned to power with a thumping majority in 1980. Though still the ruling party at the centre and in seventeen out of twenty-two states, the Congress presently appears to be in weak health. Early in 1983, party was thrown out of power in Andhra Pradesh and Karnataka, the states which were its traditional stronghold. Indeed, the Congress does not appear to be organisationally very sound. None of the 25 Pradesh Congress Committees and the 327 District Congress Committees is an elected body ; all these bodies are appointed ones. This is its serious weakness[2].

Yet there does not appear to be no other party which is strong enough to fill the gap if and when the Congress is voted out of

1. Reference is to what is presently known as the Congress (I).
2. It is common for political parties in India to persistently avoid organisational elections, thus showing scant respect for internal democracy even though externally they seek and promote democracy.

power. This aspect acquires added seriousness for another reason too. Right since the first general election, the Congress Party has been coming into power with less than fifty percent votes, and as such a swing of, say, five percent disillusioned voters is enough to knock it out of power. This entails far-reaching consequences for the country's political system, more so when analysed in the context of the following phenomena.

The Congress Party is giving way to what may be called regional parties and not to national parties. The J & K National Conference, AIADMK and Telegu Desam are, today, ruling Jammu-Kashmir, Tamil Nadu and Andhra Pradesh respectively while Akali Dal is fluttering its wings in a menacing way in Punjab. These features, namely the possible weakening of the present ruling party and the ascendancy of regionalism, are profoundly significant, and this provides the framework for the analysis of major problems which are likely to confront the Indian political system in the near future.

Regionalism as a factor in Indian politics was never totally absent, but its ascendancy is a relatively new phenomenon which is likely to subject the political system to an unprecedented level of stress. Regional parties have already established themselves in states like Andhra Pradesh, Jammu-Kashmir, Tamil Nadu etc. and are likely to be increasingly assertive in the near future. New 'revolts' against the centre are not completely unlikely in the near future and the regional pheonmena will in all probability be more assertive, fuelled also by the very style of the functioning of the Congress dominated system. Despite its safe majority in the state under its control, the Congress has itself introduced instability by its habit of centre-directed nomination of chief ministers as well as the frequent change of governments. Maharashtra has had three chief ministers since the last assembly election ; Bihar, U.P. and Rajasthan two each. It is significant that the present ruling party in Andhra Pradesh, Telegu Desam, was voted into power early in 1983 as a mark of determined popular protest against the Congress Party's style of making and unmaking chief ministers. On the positive side, the regional parties disseminate a feeling that they would be able to do something for their 'neglected' states by virtue of their unifocal loyalty and commitment. Regionalism has also acquired its present intensity from the forces which have been released from the economic sector of life in the states. The growth of capitalism in agriculture and the small scale industries has today given birth to a *noveau riche* class whose mind, quite understandably, is confined to the boundaries of their respective states. Of course, it is reinforced by factors of culture and language[3]. As already observed, the coming years are most likely to see an intensification of regionalism in India, which is apt to generate areas of tension and conflict in the political system.

It flows from the above that centre-state relations will most surely experience, high levels of imbalance in the near future. This should not be surprising in the least, for states like West Bengal and Kerala have been demanding for quite sometime a greater measure of autonomy for the states. Tamil Nadu had even set up in 1969 a Centre-State Relations Inquiry Committee under the chairmanship of R.J. Rajmannar to suggest appropriate changes in the constitution in this respect. The demand for re-structuring of centre-state relations has of late gained momentum and has become much more organised backed as it is by states presently under the rule of non-Congress parties—Andhra Pradesh, Jammu-Kashmir, Karnataka, West Bengal, Tamil Nadu etc. The gravity of the demand has been recognised by the Centre, reflected in its action to set up, in August 1983, a Commission under the chairmanship of Justice R.S. Sarkaria 'to go into centre-state relations and recommend appropriate changes within the present constitutional framework.' The centre-state relations are discussed in a separate chapter in the present work.

The office of the Governor[4] must receive serious thought. The governor's powers to appoint the chief minister and to dissolve the state legislature must be standardised to keep him beyond criticism. The present mode of his functioning makes his behaviour questionable. Immediately after the election the locus of activities relating to formation of government presently shifts to New Delhi almost as a matter of routine. Of late, the legislators seldom elect the party leader : the latter descends, like manna, from the centre, and the governor awaits a signal. No less true is the abuse of power under Article 356—the proverbial mote in the states' eye. It is significant that in most of 70-odd cases of President's rule, Article 356 has been violated in spirit.[5] Over the years the governor has become an agent

3. Regionalism is countered by several changes taking place in the country. The whole class of professionals, technicians, managers, engineers etc. which has emerged in large numbers seek or recognise no regional boundaries. The medium and higher level industrialists and traders have developed a stake in pulling down regional barriers. The chambers of commerce and industry and trade organisations, for instance, wants the sales tax to be replaced by excise duties. Similarly, many others seek unification of the national market.

4. For a detailed analysis see S.R. Maheshwari : *State Governments in India*, New Delhi, Maclmillans, 1979, pp. 220-244.

5. See S.R. Maheshwari : *President's Rule in India*, New Delhi, Macmillans. 1977.

of the central government, and it is high time he distances himself from the centre and functions in a strictly constitutional manner.

The Indian political system is characterised by one dominant party surrounded by a large number of splinter or small parties many of which plainly fall in the category of regional parties. There is thus an absence of two party or three party system, and as a consequence the opposition votes get split up, which has greatly benefited the Congress, electorally speaking. An effort was made in 1977 to evolve an alternative party in the name of the Janata Party, but this coming together of various parties with the aim of defeating the Congress was artificial and did not last beyond 1979. The other parties have been weak and small but this feature did not cause much worry as the Congress Party was always on the political scene to provide stability at both the levels of the government, especially at the central level. Today, all political parties including the Congress are in a state of disarray. Many of the parties are the lengthend shadows of individual politicians with little progammatic input. To curb mushrooming growth of political parties, the qualifying percentage of votes for recognition of parties must be raised. At present, a party which secures 4 per cent of the valid votes polled in a state is recognised as a state party while every party which performs this feat in four states is accorded the status of a national party. But there does not seem to be any political will in favour of such a move. A multiplicity of parties is thus likely to continue as a feature of the political scenario in the future as well, and all parties seem to be reconciled to it. This explains why the present emphasis appears to be on alliances rather than mergers. The alliance politics has been successfully practised by the communist parties, and the left-alliances have been successful in West Bengal and Kerala.

The formation of the multi-member United Front comprising the Janata, Congress (S), Democratic Socilist Party, Rashtriya Congress etc. and the National Democratic Alliance of the BJP and the Lok Dal indicate how the political parties are gearing themselves for the coming election. But on closer analysis this would be discovered to be a pathetic endeavour of the opposition parties to prevent splitting up of their votes. It is premature to speculate whether these two alliances would evince an abiding urge to form a broader alliance. But the prospects do not appear to be very bright. While the opposition fragmentation gets countered by these alliances, the consolidation of the opposition does not seem to be in sight. In India, politics is not yet emerging as ideology or issue-oriented ; it is deeply personality based. Or, to be more correct, politics in India is deeply election-oriented.

Elections, the gateway to political success and power, are apt to be subject to exceptionally heavy pressures in the near future if the foregoing analysis is not completely wrong. Even otherwise, electoral politics is becoming increasingly ruthless and normless in India over a period of time, and the future is most likely to see only an intensification of such trends, not their reversal unless firm and resolute reform measures are taken. The growing role of money power and the 'muscle' power as well as the mounting cost of elections should cause concern to all right-thinking citizens. The business houses with black money presently find an election a handsome opportunity to purchase political favours and no less true is the growing inter-face between politics and crime. Politics must be weaned away from such cankerous influences, and the necessary beginning has to be made with electoral reform. The election must be made cheap, and also free and fair. To reduce dependence on money power, the state should agree to subsidise contesting of elections and to this and set up an 'election fund'. As part of cleanliness in politics the political parties of the land must be obliged to maintain their accounts and get them properly audited, thereby letting the public know about their financial profiles.

The electoral administration is presently full of loopholes, which must be appropriately plugged. 'Of the four pillars of Indian democracy, namely the Supreme Court, the Public Service Commission, the Comptroller and Auditor-General of India and the Election Commission, the last is the weakest, both in conception and in practice. On closer scrutiny, it should be obvious that the strength of all these institutions, nay, of the constitutional system itself depends ultimately upon the integrity and independence of the electoral administration of the land.'[6] The Election Commission has necessarily to harness the state level adminisstrative machinery over which its control is anything but continuously in effective—as is proven by the experiences at the time of the Jammu-Kashmir assembly elections held in the summer of 1983. The Election Commisston of India needs to be strengthened constitutionally, administratively, financially and politically, failing which this body will be subjectcd to the greatest possible stress, entailing far-reaching implications for the entire polity.

A mention is often made of imbalances in the present voting principle in India which does not produce a close correspondence

6. S R. Maheshwari, 'Election Commission : Weakest Pillar of our Democracy', in *The Statesman* 18 June 1982.

between the number of votes polled and the number of seats won. This is inherent in the first-past-the post system, but a better substitute does not seem to be in sight.

AGENDA FOR ACTION

It may not thus be too rash to conclude that the immediate future is likely to be of turmoil and tension to the country's political system. Many institutions of state are to face rough weather ; and Election Commission, office of Governor, Planning Commission, all India services etc. are prominently among them and are to bear the brunt of the forces and pressures likely to be released in the nearfuture. The civil service, too, would find itself placed within a distinctly rough and tough environment, and pointed attention may be drawn to matters like postings and transfers, which are already threatening to become 'big business' in many states. Indeed, the practices being already observed in the sphere of public service are the replay, so to say, of the future scheme of things. Even what may be viewed as the basic assumptions of peaceful life are to find themselves under siege. The processes which are beginning to unfold themselves and are to unfurl themselves more completely shortly will ultimately bring about significant changes in the political (and the larger social) system, putting it on a very different keel. The political system is likely to remain fully busy with these, recently released forces, endeavouring to absorb and accommodate them.

The next general election due in the year 1985 (of not earlier) will thus be pregnant with import and meaning for the country's political system. One way of dealing with this not too distant future is to sit and wait idly till the events unfold themselves in 1985—till, in other words, the new forces burst on us with the celerity of a cyclone. Another more sensible approach is to initiate a dispassionate dialogue on the nature and shape of the political system likely to emerge after the next elections and to get ready for that future. Changes to be demanded at that time are apt to be unacceptable to all concerned for the simple reason that these would be articulated and debated under the heat of the moment. It is immensely beneficial to inaugurate a statesmanlike discussion just now in a bid to evoke a broad consensus and to initiate a process of change. Steps in this regard must be taken up within the present political frame-work itself to prove the way for its general acceptability in the future. The problems and issues identified in the present work as well as many other views and suggestions not directly listed here but nevertheless pertinent may be examined with a view to preparing an agenda for immediate action.

The planning process as ordained by the Planning Commission requires to be restructured and reformed. It must be fully realised that a decentralisation of decision-making process is overdue and inescapable. The institutions likely to be subjected to heavy stress have already been identified and consensus about their reformed structures and functions must emerge. The National Development Council must be made a more active body. The scourge of political defections must be dealt with firmly and swiftly, and the necessary legislation in this regard should brook no further delay. Corruption is nearly universal at present, and it must be checked—to avoid people's alienation from the system. Lokpal and Lokayuktas must be appointed at the earliest and accountability must be enforced at various levels of administration.

Besides, there must be a large number of autonomous institutions which may mediate between the centre and the states. A time has come when such organisations should distance themselves from the government at the centre and evolve working relationship with both the levels of government in the country. Equally necessary it is to have a viable and effective third force whose counsels may receive serious attention of all parties and politicians.

The near future for India is likely to be a period of transition, politically speaking. The traditional equilibrium is likely to get disrupted beyond restoration in its original form, but the country would need some time to stabilise a new equilibrium. The transitional period is likely to be of a measure of strife and tension, but one must not under-rate the resilience and hidden strength of the nation. It is not entirely improbable for some future national leaders of India to emerge from what are presently the regional paths. The Supreme Court of India is already becoming assertive, taking initiative and showing concern in many new matters. The press is vigorous and is relentless in exposing the dark spots in the nation's life. The crisis-managing capability of India is infinite ; and institutions and individuals will surely emerge to cope with the negative forces.

INDEX

ERRATA

Page	*Line*	*For*	*Read*
6	9	move	more
7	21	affects, its funding	affects
7	23	control, a process	control a process
8	34	minor	union
87	16	portion	part
88	4	Electoral	Election
89	5-6	provision however,	provision, however,
90	5	Finally	Fifthly
90	9	have	has